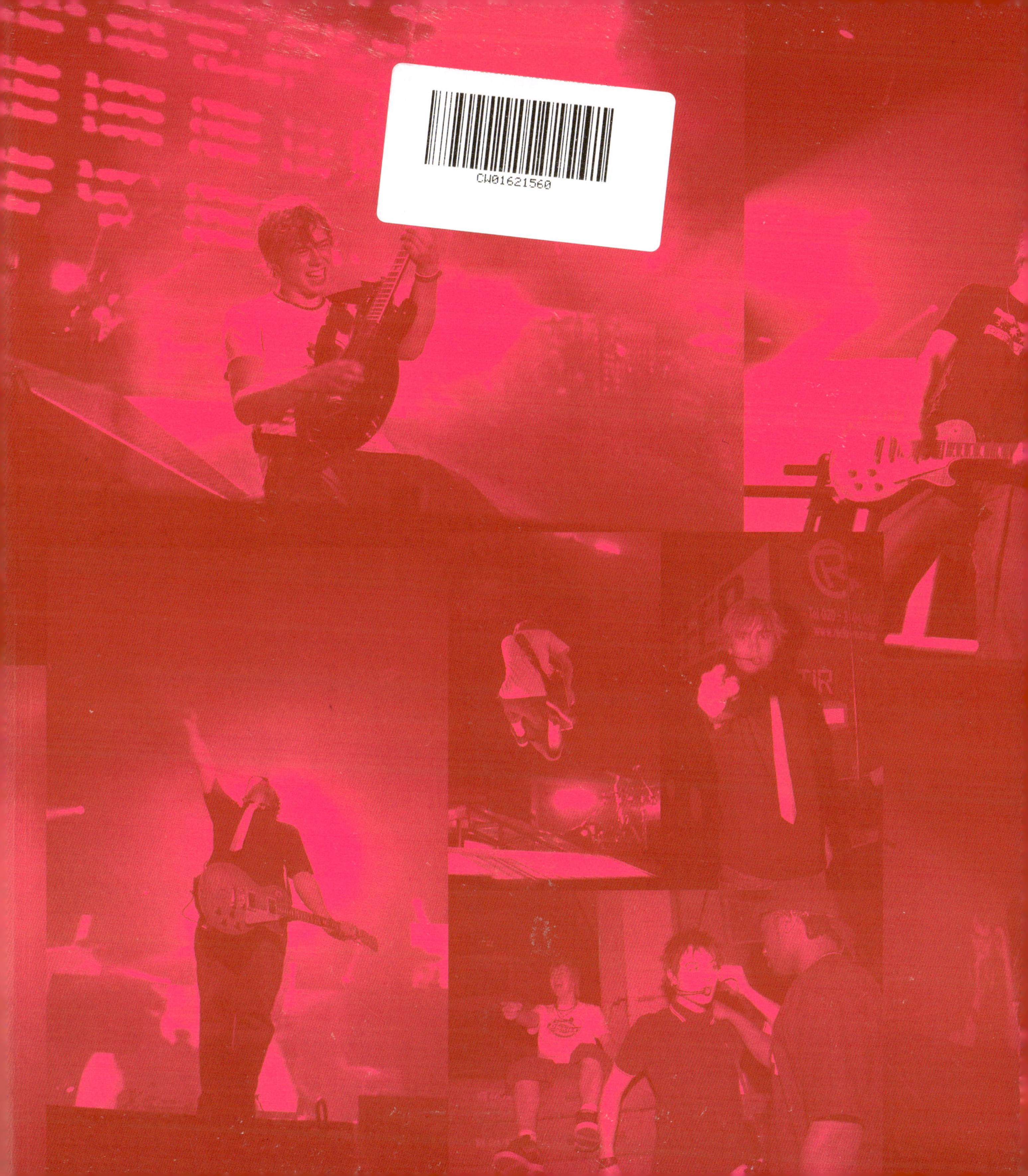

BUSTED

Busted On Tour

Peter Robinson

TED SMART

First published in Great Britain in 2004 by
Virgin Books Ltd
Thames Wharf Studios
Rainville Road
London
W6 9HA

A catalogue record for this book is available from the British Library.

This edition produced for
The Book People Ltd,
Hall Wood Avenue, Haydock,
St Helens WA11 9UL

ISBN 1 85227 256 2

Busted managed by Richard Rashman and Matt Fletcher for Prestige Management.

Art direction by Paul West at Form®
(www.form.uk.com)
Designed by Andy Harvey at Form®

Printed by The Bath Press.

Photographs:

James McMillan: 2-3, 8, 10-11, 12, 13, 14 (T-R), 15, 17 (T-R, B), 19, 21 (B), 22, 23, 25, 28, 29 (T-L, T-M, B), 30-31, 32-33, 39, 40, 41, 42, 43, 44, 45, 49, 51 (T-R), 52-53, 55, 56, 57, 58, 59, 61, 62, 63 (T-R), 64, 67, 69, 70, 71, 73, 74-75, 76-77

Ellis Parrinder at PCP Agency: 5, 7, 9, 14 (T-L), 17 (T-L), 21 (T), 27, 31,32, 47, 48, 63 (B)

Dean Chalkley/Idols Licensing and Publicity Limited: 51 (T-L)

Antony Cutajar/Idols Licensing and Publicity Limited: 18

Guy Heritage/Idols Licensing and Publicity Limited: 24, 26, 34, 35, 36, 79

Tracey Griffin/Idols Licensing and Publicity Limited: 29 (T-R)

David Tonge/Idols Licensing and Publicity Limited: 16

David Titlow/Idols Licensing and Publicity Limited: 63 (T-L)

Con-tents

Introduction

When I was first asked how I felt about spending one month on the road with the most exciting British pop group of the last five years, I said one thing: 'Haven't the Fast Food Rockers split up?'

Two weeks later I was on the Busted tour bus. With unrestricted access to the band for an entire month I found myself at the centre of the Busted whirlwind: the fan pandemonium, the 24 dates, the eight cities, the quarter of a million tickets sold, and the depressing sight of one young musician's descent into full-blown soft-cheese addiction.

'Just make us look cool,' James said, echoing a line in the movie *Almost Famous*, where a rock group are joined on the road by a journalist.

'Stop nicking lines out of films,' I said.

'Well, just write what happens, then,' he said, and that was that.

So here it is – a book about what it's really like to be on the road with one of the biggest pop groups in Britain. In one word, it's fun. But one word wouldn't make for much of a book, so read on for your very own Access All Areas pass. Just don't stand underneath any hotel windows when Matt's holding a TV.

Peter Robinson
London, April 2004

Rehear-sals

London Docklands Arena, 24 February 2004. Three o'clock in the afternoon. At the edge of the stage, James's bag is on fire. 'My bag is on fire,' he notes. 'Is that supposed to happen?'

It is not supposed to happen – James's bag is the unfortunate casualty of one pyrotechnic unexpectedly deciding to explode itself – but that is why the band are here today, in this empty arena, ironing out the creases and putting the finishing touches to their biggest live show to date. For one month Busted have been holed up at John Henry's rehearsal complex in north London – later today Charlie will admit that this has been the nearest he's ever come to a nine-to-five job – but today is their first opportunity to run through the show in the sort of venue they'll be playing for real.

James crosses the stage, stomps on his bag to put out the flames and examines the smouldering remains. The nylon has melted and the zip is stuck shut. He'll be needing a new bag for the tour.

Tickets first went on sale almost a year ago, before the band's first album, *Busted*, sold its millionth copy and long before their second album, *A Present For Everyone*, sold as many copies in its first three weeks as *Busted* did in its entire chart run. In the time since last spring's national theatre tour, Busted have gone from being the brightest hopes on the pop block to household names, and are arguably the biggest pop band in the country. To begin with, only seven dates were announced for this tour; when they began selling out, more dates were added. And then *more* dates were added. Eventually the *A Ticket For Everyone* tour had notched up 24 sold-out arena dates.

The boys have been deep in preparation for the tour, and their priorities are as straight as ever. No bags have been packed, but James and Charlie have been feverishly loading songs into their respective iPods. Matt, meanwhile, has simply thrown all his CDs into a bag and will drag them with him from venue to venue.

Over a takeaway lunch, the band take one final look over the set list. Right now, it looks like this: 'Air Hostess', 'That Thing You Do', 'What I Go To School For', 'She Wants To Be Me', '3am', 'Why', 'Loner In Love', 'Who's David', 'Teenage Kicks', 'Better Than This', then a sequence in which Charlie will perform a drum solo, followed by a cover of Black Eyed Peas' 'Where Is The Love?', 'Fake', 'Nerdy' and 'You Said No'. The encore will consist of three songs: 'Year 3000', 'Sleeping With The Light On' and finally 'Crashed

0000 240304

ATFE

CTW 101003

***

Aeroporto

VIA Dublin/ Belfast/ Newcastle/ Nottingham/ Birmingham/ Sheffield/ Cardiff/ London/ Glasgow/ Manchester/

***

BSTD

DESTINATION

BUSTED

Rehear-sals

'That was awesome,' Charlie declares. 'I can't wait to do it for real.'

The Wedding', at the end of which the band will each jump through a hole in the stage and disappear from view.

'We totally knew from the word go that "Air Hostess" had to be the opening track,' Matt explains: 'If only because of the amazing "Do do do do do do" intro. From that point onwards we had to place our singles strategically throughout the set, and then pick out which album tracks and B-sides we wanted to play. What's great is that when we're doing them live, some of the album tracks, like "3am", sound just as good as the singles.'

'It's great to feel the show coming together,' Charlie agrees. He admits now that, on Busted's first tour, 'We really didn't have a clue what we were doing. The learning curve was unbelievably steep. This time it seems we're more on top of things.' James nods. 'I look back on the theatre tour and I think that it didn't really sound that good,' he adds, 'and this is our chance to make everything sound *brilliant*. Also, of course, we've got twice as much material now so there's no weak point in the set, whereas on the first tour I think we were a bit stuck for a few songs to play.'

Milling around today are some faces we'll be seeing a lot of over the next month. Up on the stage are the three extra musicians who'll be joining James, Matt and Charlie on stage each night: drummer Damon, keyboardist (and occasional bassist) Chris Banks and third guitarist Chris Leonard. Chatting in the corner are Busted's management team, Matt Fletcher (Fletch, to avoid confusion) and Richard Rashman, and, with a woolly hat pulled down over his face and a mobile phone clamped to his ear, we also find Adam Lambert, Busted's tour manager. Adam's job is to make sure things happen when the schedule says they should happen; without Adam the tour simply wouldn't happen at all.

After lunch the stage is cleared and the band run through the gig, in full, for the very first time. It's a spectacular show, from the moment the boys magically appear from below the stage for 'Air Hostess' to the final, screeching feedback of the last few seconds of 'Crashed The Wedding', and it captures perfectly everything which makes Busted Britain's most innovative pop band. Afterwards, the boys are ecstatic. 'That was awesome,' Charlie declares. 'I can't wait to do it for real.'

He won't have to wait long – in two days we'll be in Dublin for the first night.

Dublin

February 26

The band's white, double-level tour bus is waiting outside the hotel, chugging and ready to go. Having checked into his room, Charlie is the first to emerge from the hotel's glass revolving doors – big, green coat, hat pulled down over his eyes, sandwich in hand, ready for action. He jumps on the bus and takes a look around: at the wood-effect sideboards, the well-stocked fruit bowl, the on-board toilet (into which, Charlie insists, there will be deposited no solids), the plump leather seats. 'This,' he declares, dropping some sandwich on the carpet, 'is a nice tour bus.'

It's just as well. For Charlie, Matt and James this bus will be the nearest thing to home over the next month, as they visit ten cities around the British Isles. Charlie's obviously excited at the prospect of going on tour, and bounds up the steep stairwell to check out the bunks and second seating area. 'It's more a case of it being a nice, and rather large, taxi,' he decides. 'A taxi in which you can sometimes sleep. I always get a good sleep on tour buses.'

Before long James and – only a little late – Matt join us on the bus, the door slides itself shut and we begin our journey to Dublin's Point Depot, the scene for tonight and tomorrow's gigs. Time for more exploration, this time with the whole band clambering around the bus. It is swiftly established that one of the seats in the upstairs lounge will be, in Matt's words, 'the captain's chair'.

'This,' he says, 'is where the referee sits when we are playing Connect 4.' It is worth noting that, if you believe Connect 4 to be a game that requires no referee, you have never experienced the heated arguments that occur when Matt and Charlie are playing. A paperback copy of *Killing Pablo* ('the hunt for the richest, most powerful criminal in history', apparently) lies unread on the counter. Perhaps wisely, nobody admits ownership of the book.

After a twenty-minute drive, during which the boys carry out a full inspection of the tour bus minibar (some cans of Coke, some water and, for after the show, rather a lot of beer), we pull up at The Point, drive through a set of sturdy,

fan-flanked gates and stop in the backstage parking area. Before the bus door opens, Adam Lambert opens his bag and pulls out a fistful of yellow, Access All Areas tour laminates, each with a name on the back. These will be given to every member of the Busted tour party, and they must not be lost. We pull them over our heads and troop through the stage door to Busted's dressing room.

On the dressing table, we find the following: one box of man-size Kleenex, two tubs of Toni & Guy hair product (one Funky Gum, one Shine-Glaze), one tub of VO5 Texturing Gum, one packet of cushioned plasters, one can of Ellnette hairspray, one packet of Nurofen, some Revlon Colorstay foundation, a tube of Garnier 2-in-1 dandruff shampoo, some Radox shower gel, a tin of Sure For Men Active Response deodorant, a tube of Gillette shaving gel, a tub of Vaseline, a tube of Colgate Total Advance toothpaste, a tube of Berocca vitamin and mineral tablets, some effervescent double-action Vitamin C + Zinc tablets, a tube of Boots effervescent Echinacea, a packet of witch hazel and tea tree cleaning and toning wipes, three toothbrushes (all clearly marked James, Matt and Charlie), red Gillette razors marked Charlie and James, 24 Vocalzone throat lozenges

'This,' declares James, 'is our best video so far.'

and six blue towels. These items – along with the band's requested rider – will be in the dressing room on every night of the tour.

Before long, it's time for the first soundcheck. This is a routine the band will go through for every date over the next month – playing tracks from the set to check everything's working both on stage and halfway back in the arena, on the sound desk where musical director Gareth Brown will be controlling what comes out of the PA. The band run through 'Air Hostess', 'She Wants To Be Me' and 'Crashed The Wedding'. Everyone seems happy, so Busted retire once again to their dressing room. Here they are handed a rough edit of the video to 'Air Hostess'. They'd filmed the video three weeks ago in between tour rehearsals, and the post-production – swapping green screens for footage of airport runways, and so on – is still in progress back in London. At one point, when an exterior shot shows the plane spinning 360° in the sky, the screen goes completely black, except for the words 'PLANE 360' spinning around.

'We should keep it like that,' Matt announces. 'It would be the world's cheapest special effect.'

'This,' declares James, 'is our best video so far.'

It is agreed that 'Air Hostess' is certainly better than the video for 'Who's David', mention of which prompts a series of groans from the band. It was boring, says Charlie. It featured female acrobats for no reason whatsoever, adds Matt, who also suffered the ignominy of having to use the same phone box in the 'Who's David' video as in the 'Sleeping With The Light On' clip. 'It did rather seem as if someone

'Listen to that.' Matt grins. 'They're going to be screaming for us later.'

had decided that, whenever Busted do a song which isn't about air hostesses getting off with teachers at a wedding in the year 3000, I have to stand looking pensive in a phone box,' he adds. 'Not just a phone box. The phone box. The Matt From Busted Phone Box Of Moodiness.'

Another part of the daily on-the-road routine is catering. Catering is where dinner happens. But dinner is not called dinner, it is called catering. The boys decide to go for catering at 6 p.m., half an hour before the doors open.

During the first course, James pauses and stares at Matt.

James: Matt, you're eating very weirdly today.

Matt: How?

James: I don't know. It's just your *mouth*. It's weird.

Charlie: I don't like this soup.

James: What is it?

Charlie: Potato and leek.

Matt: But you don't like leek.

Charlie: Yeah, I know.

Matt: I don't eat weirdly, do I?

At 7.30 p.m. we hear the first screams of the tour: the warm up is beginning. 'Listen to that.' Matt grins. 'They're going to be screaming for us later.'

While McFly are on stage, Busted are getting ready in their dressing room and there's a moment, a couple of minutes before the band make their way to the stage, when Charlie's regular nonchalant persona slips slightly to reveal an 18-year-old musician thrilled at the idea of going on stage. Any first-night nerves seem to have been superseded by a feeling of utter exhilaration, and from the moment the band first appear on stage – to an audience response Matt will later claim is among the loudest of his career so far – they're in their element. The number '3am' is incendiary tonight, and Matt's solo spot establishes 'Better Than This' as an unexpected audience favourite.

After the show we pause for a short while in the dressing room then grab our stuff, jump back onto the tour bus and drive back to the hotel to freshen up before heading out on the town. There's another gig tomorrow night, but the band agree to allow themselves a few drinks in a swank club called Lily's Bordello – which sounds rather more outré than it actually is, and is well known in rock and pop circles as the ideal destination for an after-show drink. By 1 a.m. the drink is flowing freely and a toast is made to the first date of the tour.

Then Bono from U2 arrives, and we have to give him our seats.

February 27

Dublin

On the tour bus, James is in a bad mood. Flicking through a car magazine two months ago he had seen a Delorean – the exact model used in the original *Back To The Future* films, with the doors that flap up in the air like wings – for sale, but hesitated about buying it on two grounds. Firstly, he still hasn't passed his driving test. Secondly, the house he was living in at the time didn't have a garage or even a parking space and James felt that leaving a time machine like one in a film he'd seen sat on the roadside was slightly absurd. In the time since, he's bought a new house – with a parking space – but he's just heard that the Delorean has been sold. 'Those cars,' he mopes, 'are as rare as rocking-horses***. I don't want a Porsche, and I will not be getting an X5. Deloreans are a far more elite car than that.'

Are they practical?

'No, not at all. I'm not a very practical person. But when I watched *Back To The Future* again the other day I suddenly realised that Deloreans were the reason I'd wanted to drive. Literally, the *only* reason.'

From the stairwell, Matt points out that James seems not to have taken into account the fact that the Delorean he eventually buys will, in all likelihood, have difficulty travelling through time.

'I know,' James says, a little unhappily. 'I know this. But as long as those doors spring up and I can dress it up to make it look like the one in the film, I'll be happy. I'll get some smoke machines put in the back.'

Why don't you get a Tannoy installed on the top, someone suggests, so you can drive around going, 'Look, I'm James out of Busted and I'm driving the car from *Back To The Future*'?

'Perhaps. It would be so cool to go back down to Southend and to drive down the road with the film soundtrack blaring out of the window. So next time I see one I'm going to buy it, park it in my new parking space, and leave it there until I can drive it.'

'In typical James fashion,' Matt snorts, 'the first things he moved into the house were his platinum discs.' James shrugs his shoulders and pulls one of his trademark well-you've-got-to-haven't-you-really expressions.

'I think what you should do in your house is knock the stairs down,' Fletch helpfully chirps, 'and get a fireman's pole.'

'Robbie Williams had a fireman's pole,' James retorts, and the topic is closed.

As the band's rider is laid out in the dressing room, Matt reflects on the first night's show and how it differed from playing to much smaller audiences on last year's theatre tour.

'I didn't expect it to be so different,' he admits. 'It seems much harder to connect with an audience on this scale. And then of course you feel like you're *trying* to connect with them, when you shouldn't be trying to do anything other than what comes naturally.' Still, he adds, it seems to be going all right so far. 'To get people so far back as involved as the people at the front is a real challenge, but people right at the back and up the sides often seem to get into the show much more than the people at the front.'

During tonight's show, and despite another thorough soundcheck, there is a repeat of some niggling problems from last night. Occasionally guitars will cut out during songs, and some of the guitars that have been tuned before the show have become mysteriously out-of-tune by the time they go on stage. It is agreed that this must be sorted out before tomorrow night's show in Belfast.

On the way back to the hotel we stop off at a service station for some supplies and everyone piles off the bus. As ever with Busted, the

'Look, I'm James out of Busted and I'm driving the car from *Back To The Future.*'

escapade takes twice as long as is strictly necessary. Matt refuses to leave until he has inspected the CD rack which, as is often the case in petrol stations, stocks nothing but mid-price CD compilations aimed at people who spend a lot of their time driving, alone, on long, dark motorways. He flicks his way through the CDs – *20 Truckin' Hits*, *Keep On Truckin'* and so on – and for a brief moment looks as if he is considering making a purchase.

Back at the hotel the boys have three drinks in the bar before calling it a night and heading off to bed. Tomorrow we will leave early to travel to Belfast, check in to another hotel, and do this all over again. Adam explains that 'leaving early' seems to mean a 1 p.m. wake-up call for the band.

'I think,' Matt announces as he stops the lift doors from sliding shut, 'that I could get used to that sort of early start.' And he heads back to the bar.

February 28

Belfast

Matt flings the door open and waves his still uneaten steak around on a fork.

Snow lines the ground outside Belfast's Culloden Hotel, but the sun is shining. Down the road local kids are so bored that they're on a petrol station forecourt breathing in the compressed air, and outside the hotel a group of fans have written 'Busted rock' in the snow. But Busted are not the hotel's only special guests this weekend. One couple have chosen the hotel to host their wedding reception, and in the toilet two of the groom's friends discuss the pop stars who have – and there are various unamusing comments made about this over the course of the next two days – crashed the wedding.

'I'm a closet fan,' says one.

'I've never heard of them,' says the other, as he splashes his shoe.

While the band sign autographs for some waiting fans in reception, the wedding guests – one of whom Matt will later identify as having sported 'the very worst haircut of all time' – mill around and get drunk.

Hung over and hungry, Matt brings his room-service lunch – a massive steak – onto the bus, complete with china plate and sterling-silver cutlery. After two bites he pronounces himself full and casts the plate aside, virtually untouched.

We arrive at Belfast's Odyssey Arena at 4 p.m. As the bus drives through the electronic gates and past a group of fifty or so fans, Matt flings the door open and waves his still uneaten steak around on a fork. 'Who wants some of my meat?' he bellows, prompting a massive scream.

I mention that on the Internet auction site eBay right now someone is offering what they claim to be 'Busted soap' – a bar of Imperial Leather purportedly salvaged from a hotel room used by the band. A little disconcertingly, the seller promises that the soap comes 'with one hair attached'. There have already been three bids. Matt, for once, is speechless.

This afternoon's soundcheck is another opportunity to iron out the problems of the first two nights' shows, principally involving Charlie's guitar, which has developed a habit of cutting out during 'What I Go To School For'. Everything seems to be in order by 7.30 p.m. and, as Charlie and Damon practise their drum-off in the corner, the atmosphere in the dressing room is beginning to build once again.

Throughout the afternoon, staff at the Arena have painstakingly flyered each and every one of the 10,000 seats with a slip of paper informing audience members that under no circumstances are they to stand up during the performance. Charlie has already branded the rule 'utter bollocks' and on stage, after 'What I Go To School For', James addresses the issue. 'It's nice,' he begins, 'to see so many people standing up.' In the audience, confusion reigns. Some fans see this as permission to leave their seats; others, who've ignored the requests of the Arena and are already standing up, think it is a hint to sit down. 'Stand up!' James eventually shouts.

Not everything goes so smoothly. The problems with Charlie's guitar in 'What I Go To School For' have been solved tonight, but have been replaced by many more hitches. During 'Teenage Kicks', James's own guitar malfunctions so badly in the first verse that he has to run off stage for a replacement, leaving Matt to fill in his lines, and James only makes it back to his microphone in time for Charlie's verse. Similar problems plague the rest of the show, and in the four minutes between 'You Said No' and the encore the band are fuming.

After the show they storm through the corridor and shut themselves in their dressing room. This is Busted being Not At All Happy. Through the closed door you can make out James muttering something about how Formula One drivers don't have to sit in the pit for three minutes

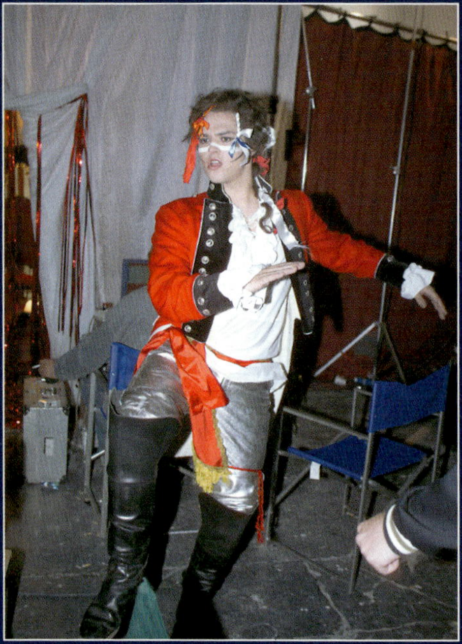

waiting for their tyres to be changed. Charlie is swearing a lot. (Though, to be fair, Charlie is always swearing a lot.) To make matters even worse, tonight's has been the first show to be watched by the support acts, and Busted feel they've embarrassed themselves in front of their support acts. From behind the door a series of complaints are hurled around for fifteen minutes, but when the door opens, the situation has been diffused. At least, someone optimistically suggests, it's not the same show every night.

'Why couldn't it have been as good as last night?' Matt wonders, open palmed.

There is silence for thirty seconds, until Charlie finally answers, in typically playful Charlie manner: 'Well actually, I thought last night was shit.'

Back at the hotel, the wedding party, which has been here all afternoon and now all evening, is generously lubricated. Matt goes to his room to get changed and calm his nerves – his sixteen-year-old sister watched tonight's show, and will soon be introducing him to her new boyfriend for the first time – and when he returns he is immediately collared by the bride, who broadcasts the fact that she is 'more nervous about meeting Busted than I was about getting married'. She goes on to thank Matt for making her day. Which, as Matt will later observe, is a rum old statement to make on your wedding day.

'Why couldn't it have been as good as last night?' Matt wonders, open palmed.

After a short spell at the bar, Adam persuades the hotel manager to open up a function room for the Busted party. The manager reluctantly shows us into a special room, but warns us that we must not make a mess and must not spill any drinks, since the room has already been set for something very important tomorrow morning. This noted, James sets about spraying the room with champagne, because that is what rock stars – and Formula One drivers whose tyres have been changed quickly enough – sometimes do. The champagne has barely settled on the tablecloths, luxurious shag pile

and assembled members of the Busted touring crew before the manager storms back in and gives James an unceremonious bollocking in front of everyone. Against James's wishes, the ground refuses to open up and swallow him.

At 3.30 a.m., James invites us up to his room to listen to a new Busted song. This is one of those hotel rooms whose lights only work when a key card is inserted in a slot where the light switch should be. Having lost the appropriate card, James stumbles around in the dark, finds a knife and jams it in the hole. The lights come on – a happy consequence, seeing as the alternative was electrocution.

While he rummages through piles of caseless CDs and CD-less cases – none of which seem to correspond – he reflects on his champagne-related telling-off.

'It was only when we got in there that he said, "Oh, don't spill any drink." I was like, "C'mon, if you're partying in a room, then drinks are gonna get spilled." And that is exactly what happened.' Eventually James finds the CD he's looking for and slides it into the hotel room stereo. As it whirrs its way to the beginning of the song, he announces: 'This is one of the best songs Busted have ever recorded.'

The song – 'Thunderbirds Are Go' – will soundtrack the main title sequence of the forthcoming Hollywood version of the 1960s puppet show. At the end of last year the film's production company, Working Title (who've also worked on movies like *Love, Actually* and *Bridget Jones' Diary*) approached Busted with a view to recording a song for the film. They showed James, Matt and Charlie some rough footage from the movie and the result is now blaring around James's hotel room, through an open window and out into the icy Belfast hill tops.

The spilled champagne is still playing on James's mind. 'Oh God.' He grimaces. 'The whole thing's just reminded me of when I was ten years old, and I bashed my friend's head against the wall at school.'

By accident?

'No, I was having a fight with him.' He laughs. 'But his mum was in the playground and just stood there yelling at me for ten minutes. I was sent to the head's office for further punishment and he was eating an apple. Every time he yelled something at me a little bit of apple hit me in the face.'

February 29

Belfast

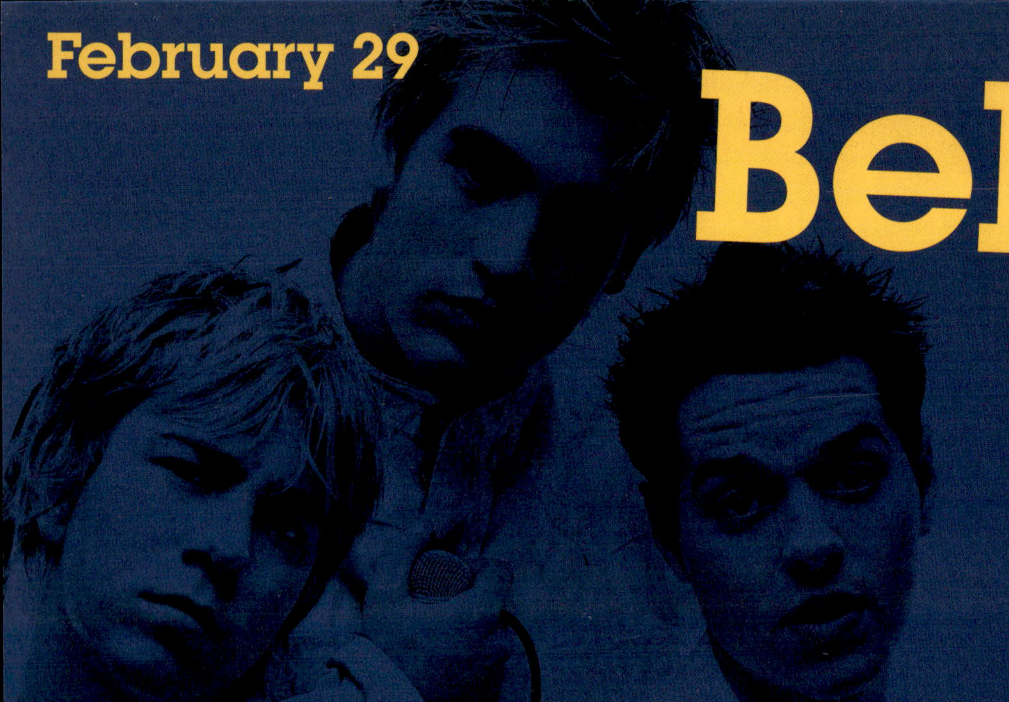

Sunday afternoon on the tour bus. Charlie and James nurse their hangovers as Matt brews some foul-smelling herbal tea that, he tells us proudly, is the same tea Madonna drinks when she's on tour. James is wrestling with the bus's built-in CD player. 'How does this work?' he wails.

'You leave it,' Matt retorts, 'to someone who knows what they're doing.' He presses the 'On' button and the system springs to life. The band listen to 'Thunderbirds Are Go' twice. There are two different versions – the fourteenth and fifteenth reswizzles – on the CD, which was sent direct from the studio last week. On the fifteenth, the guitars are a little higher in the mix. After it has finished, Matt sits in silence for a short while. 'I know that this is the point when I'm supposed to debate the merits of both versions,' he says. 'I know I'm supposed to say how much better these versions sound than versions eight and nine. But, to be quite honest, I can't even tell the difference. Is there a bit more trumpet in it now?' After a while, he adds, 'I preferred the first mix.'

During the soundcheck at Odyssey Arena, Charlie mistakenly lets rip a cry of 'Hello Dublin!'

'Hello Spain!' yells James.

'Hello Reigate!' Charlie concludes.

The band play a bit of the Red Hot Chili Peppers' 'Californication'.

Afterwards, they discuss last night's problems, and the previous night's problems, and the *previous* night's problems, with Skirmish, the tour's main guitar tech. Strings keep breaking, Fletch contributes. Shit happens, Skirmish shrugs. I need a new guitar, James decides. One of the guitar pedals is too far away from the mic stand, Charlie adds. The guitars keep going out of tune for 'Teenage Kicks', Matt notes. The problems are noted and the band return to their PlayStation.

In spite of last night's stand-up protest, the venue staff have once again flyered each seat with strict instructions for the audience to remain seated. Nonetheless, Busted's show tonight is the best so far – the problems experienced last night and in Dublin have been solved, and the result is a massive boost to the band's confidence that makes, for the first time, for a blazing live show.

Tonight is also the first time the entire *A Ticket For Everyone* entourage share the same hotel bar drinks. All three bands sit in a large circle and drinks flow until 3 a.m. It is just as well, Richard Rashman notes, that tomorrow is a day off.

The next time we see each other, we'll all be in Newcastle.

During the soundcheck at Odyssey Arena, Charlie mistakenly lets rip a cry of 'Hello Dublin!'

March 2

Newcastle

"Do you like Busted? If you want to be cool, get into Busted."

Backstage at the Newcastle Arena, James reveals that, in a rather unusual turn of events, he's been chatting on the phone with legendary Rolling Stones guitarist Ronnie Wood, who has expressed an interest in working with Busted. James explains how it all came about.

'I know a guy called Paul, who's an old friend of my dad's. Paul is Ronnie's brother-in-law and one day, when Ronnie was visiting, Paul's son was like, "Do you like Busted? If you want to be cool, get into Busted."' James laughs at the idea of Ronnie Wood being lectured on cool. 'But Ronnie heard some of our stuff and decided that he wanted to collaborate with us!

'I got Ronnie's number off Paul and phoned him up. He went, "Oh, hello, James!" and was really nice on the phone. It was so weird. He's such a household name, this guy who I spent loads of money on to see play live, and there I was speaking to him on the phone. I said, "Is this nonsense about you wanting to collaborate with the band?" and he was like, "No, it's not. I really want to do something." He said that there was an old Fats Domino song called "Busted" that he wanted to do with us.'

Do you look at that as a real seal of approval?

'Yes, yes it does seem that way. Because there are some people who write us off as a young band, and occasionally, when you get people like Ronnie Wood who want to collaborate, it feels quite vindicating in a way.'

Talk turns to one of Busted's favourite topics – credibility. Whether they have it, whether they want it, who else has it, whether it's worth having. Since the band first emerged in the late summer of 2002 they've scored a string of hit singles and sold millions of albums, but from the word go there were question marks in some quarters over whether they were a real band or not. There was no drummer, which seemed to confuse some people, and there is still some doubt that the band are everything they say they are.

Do you think that because of the way you've been marketed, which is as a mainstream pop act, people immediately assume a certain degree of talentlessness?

'Yeah, I guess, but we *are* a mainstream pop act. The thing is that, because everyone out there has watched *Pop Idol* and *Fame Academy*, they like to think they know how the music business works. So because of that they think that when they see us in *Smash Hits* that means that we don't write and we don't play.'

I suggest that, at the beginning, it was difficult to believe that the music Busted were playing really was written by a group of teenagers. The structure of the lyrics and the music just seemed too studied, too perfect.

'A lot of people have said that. Then again other people go, "I watched you on TV and you were obviously

'If you're going to break a guitar, break a guitar spectacularly,' James advises.

miming because your hands didn't even change position on your guitar." It's, like, that's because all of our songs are written on three chords – the reasons my hands don't move is because I'm only moving one finger to drop the chord down to a D, then moving two fingers down a string to get to a C. So people criticise our ability to play music when they clearly can't hear how it was written – or even how it should look when it's played live – so I don't get too worked up about it.'

Wouldn't you say that there's still a manufactured element to the way you were first presented, though? You were in school uniforms. You didn't wear them around the house, did you? Do you see how people still find it difficult to believe that as a band you aren't just as stylised now?

'The distinction which I think makes us a real band rather than a manufactured band is that we were a band before we had a record deal; we went round all the record labels playing songs we'd written ourselves, acoustically, and in the end we went for a record deal which wasn't offering the most money but one which was offering us the best opportunity to develop as artists and as songwriters. I'm not sure that on any of those counts there's a more credible way of having gone about any of it.' It's been noted that you would probably have gained respect more quickly if you'd all been pig-ugly.

'Yeah.' James laughs. 'It's interesting. Everyone always goes, "Well, you're really successful because you look good," and I just say, "Name me an ugly star." How many ugly famous people can you think of? The most credible artists – Chris Martin from Coldplay, the Strokes, the White Stripes – these are all good-looking people. There are no ugly superstars.'

A crew from German pop magazine *Bravo* are here to shoot some behind-the-scenes pictures with the band. Germany is one of Busted's biggest markets outside the UK – so popular, in fact, that last year the German branch of Universal Records persuaded the band to record a frankly bizarre song called 'Hurra, Hurra, Die Schule Brennt' ('Hurrah, Hurrah, The School Is On Fire') as a single. The song is an old pop classic back in Germany, and lyrics go: 'Their lips are blue, hair is green, they got piercings in their ears / Sticking it out of pockets, some bottles of beer / They're running through the streets and every place that they go / Is a stench of fuel in the air'. Perhaps wisely the single was not elected for release as a UK single, though it did turn up as a 'Crashed The Wedding' B-side. Before the show, talk has turned to the band's guitars. When they leave the stage at the end of the very final song, 'Crashed The Wedding', they run to the top of the stage set and jump through a hole in the floor and on to crash mats, but before they do that their guitars are placed very carefully on the floor. There has been some debate over whether there is any place for Being Very Careful in a rock show.

'If you're going to break a guitar, break a guitar spectacularly,' James advises. 'But if you're not going to break it, put it down carefully. You can't do it halfway. I like my guitar. Someone spent a lot of time making it, and I hate waste.'

'Yes, you see that's the problem,' Charlie agrees. 'It's the fact that I have a nice guitar and I don't want to break it.'

'I don't think anyone's suggesting we drive over our guitars in a steamroller,' Matt says. 'But we could just sort of...drop them on the stage. So it looks a bit less like we're working in a museum.'

'But I'd rather just put mine down,' Charlie says. 'I do have the best guitar.'

'Shame you don't know how to play it,' James teases.

'Yeah,' Matt says, guffawing, 'and that you've got a small penis.'

March 3

Notting-ham

For the band, the memory of that Brits night is one they'll keep with them for a long time.

On the boys' first night in each of the cities they visit, a meet-and-greet session has been organised by the local promoters. Busted have taken part in hundreds of these events over the past couple of years, and during tonight's the band have been given a home-made booklet entitled 'The Busted Fan Annual 2003–2004'. As well as some odd topless photos of James it includes a page covering the 2004 Brit Awards. It contains two photographs, both captioned and time-stamped. The first reads '1 p.m. – Sober', the second '1 a.m. – Drunk'. In many ways this analysis of the boys' Brits day is as honest and as in-depth as anyone could possibly offer.

For the band, the memory of that Brits night is one they'll keep with them for a long time.

'We seriously didn't expect to win anything,' Charlie remembers. It's generally assumed in many circles that award winners are informed in advance that they've scooped a prize, but this year – at least in Busted's case – they had no idea. 'I really couldn't see how we could possibly beat the people who we did beat in those two categories. I didn't see how Justin Timberlake wouldn't win Best Pop, or the Darkness wouldn't win Best Breakthrough, especially since Best Breakthrough was voted by Radio One listeners.'

You've talked a lot about how important it was that both the Brits you won were decided by a public vote.

'Yes, it's absolutely amazing.'

Don't you also crave recognition from the industry, though? The bigwigs and suits who vote for the other awards?

'Maybe. But the industry voters made the wrong decisions anyway – the Darkness are nice guys but Muse should have won Best British Rock Group and Radiohead should have won Best British Band.'

Charlie rummages around in the bowl of sweets supplied on the dressing-room rider and among the daily Haribo allowance finds a huge, ten-centimetre-long blue gummy dolphin. As he dangles it in his mouth one of the touring crew – the wonderfully named Holly Day – notices and tries to stop him.

'But it'll give you constipation!' she shrieks.

'Why?' Charlie huffs.

'Well, just look at it!'

Charlie stuffs it in his mouth whole and makes his way to an interview – with the Spanish teen magazine, *Loka*, and its editor, Alvaro Garcia.

Alvaro: Now, I have a funny question...

Did you know that James has been wearing those trousers every day on the tour, and they still haven't been washed?

Charlie: Ooh, a funny one...

Alvaro: How long have you ever been without a shower?

Matt: Did you know that James has been wearing those trousers every day on the tour, and they still haven't been washed?

James: But they don't smell.

Matt: THAT DOESN'T MEAN THEY'RE CLEAN!

Alvaro: Would you participate in *Pop Idol*?

All: No.

Alvaro: If you had three questions to ask a genie, what would they be?

Charlie: I'd ask to be able to fly, and to have eternal happiness...

Matt: But the problem there, Charlie, is that that is *pretend* happiness.

Charlie: It would be real though.

Matt: No it wouldn't! So, you'd wake up in bed one morning having been stabbed and you'd be like, 'I don't care because I'm so eternally happy'?

Charlie: Good point. Maybe I'd just go for having a really good immune system. Take the 'Happiness' off the list. I'll make *myself* happy, thank you very much.

Matt: Now you're wasting your genie!

The questions turn to sex, and the band are asked how old they were when they lost their respective virginities. 'So,' Matt says, turning to Alvaro, 'when did you lose *your* virginity?'

'When I was eighteen,' comes the reply.

'Eighteen?! I thought you were all supposed to be randy in Spain.' Matt flicks through one of Alvaro's magazines for evidence. In Europe, teen pop magazines have a far more relaxed approach to sex and will often feature full-frontal nudity and breathtakingly graphic cartoon strips among the posters of new pop acts, but even Matt is shocked about what he finds in *Loka*. Over two pages is a practical how-to guide concerning an eyebrow-raising sexual act that is still illegal in many parts of the world.
'Oh my goodness,' Matt shrieks. 'Oh. My. GOODNESS!'

'Yes,' Alvaro concedes, the evidence seemingly against him. 'I suppose I was quite late.'

With the interview over, Charlie confides that he has been experiencing some strange dreams while on tour. Recurring instances involve Charlie being shot, stabbed and electrocuted. 'The blood,' he moans, 'always feels really warm. The other night I dreamed I was in a cab going to my new house. There were some guys looking dodgy in the street and, as I handed a £20 note over to the cab driver, the window smashed and a gun was held to my face.'

What do you think that says about your life?

'That I'm scared of being held up at gunpoint while paying for a cab.'

Birmingham

In last year's *Busted: The Official Book*, James, Charlie and Matt recalled moving into their London flat for the first time. It was two weeks before they signed their record deal, and they remembered that it was 'like some sort of pop theme park', with loads of other bands all living in flats in the same complex. Matt and Charlie have since moved out but James has now bought his own place here. That's what the flats are like: tenants come and go. Some, like Fletch, live here for years, while others, like the various bands and pop stars who've resided here over the last five years, leave for pastures new when they can afford manors of their own, or for pastures less expensive when everything goes tits up and their bank managers suggest that it really would be a better idea all round if they considered moving to a well-appointed cardboard box.

The tour bus is outside the apartment block, chugging away, waiting for Charlie and Matt to arrive. At 1 p.m., it will leave for Birmingham but Jim, Busted's driver, seems concerned that the A406 is at a standstill. Fortunately Adam, who's been here all morning, knows a cheeky route out of London.

James is the first on the Busted bus, clambering aboard and provoking gasps of both amazement and horror with a wildly unkempt hairstyle flapping around in the breeze. As Matt observes when he arrives five minutes later, 'James, don't bother saying anything because I cannot take you seriously with your hair like that. You look like a cross between a Bee Gee, a lion and that bloke off *Bargain Hunt*.' As Matt begins to unpack his bag (prize finds: a Queens Of The Stone Age CD and a Sherbet Dip Dab), James observes that Matt has become more well spoken during his time in the band.

'Well,' Matt replies, 'I *am* surrounded by posh people.'

The band talk music.

Matt: I'm not sure what to make of Dave Grohl's new *Probot* CD.

Charlie: I saw the new Hundred Reasons album in HMV last week. I looked at it and said to myself, 'I'm not going to buy that CD.' And I didn't.

James: I'm looking forward to hearing Avril Lavigne's new album. I'm going to write some songs for her...But under a different name. (Matt puts on the Ludacris album.)

Charlie: Hip-hop is shit.

Matt: No it's not.

Charlie: It's bloody rubbish.

James: I think your problem, Charlie, is that you can't get your

head around it because you can't play it on a guitar.

Matt: But we're playing 'Where Is The Love?' on tour, with our guitars.

James: But hip-hop is more a studio creation, rather than an on-stage one.

Charlie: Hip-hop is shit.

We stop at a service station for food, drink and those bodily functions banned from the tour bus toilet. Before he steps off the bus, Charlie reaches for his woolly hat and pulls it down almost over his eyes – and certainly over his eyebrows – as part of what he describes as 'my cunning disguise'. So cunning is this disguise that the first teenagers to spot Charlie immediately recognise him and demand an autograph as, ironically, a disguise-free Matt and James saunter past and into the service station. Once inside, Charlie has an inept run-in with a cash dispenser in which he enters the wrong PIN number in the first instance and has his card returned on the second attempt, on account of it being totally incompatible with the machine. He asks Adam if he can borrow some cash. 'Here's fifty pounds,' Adam says, handing Charlie a well-worn £20 note. 'Make sure you pay me back later.' Charlie nods, says a polite thank you and trots off in the direction of KFC, oblivious to the fact that, when he does repay Adam £50, he'll be £30 down.

The dressing room at the Birmingham NEC seems slightly smaller than others on the tour. Blue-and-white flecked carpet lines the floor and three large black leather sofas face inwards; one framed art print on the wall, titled 'Birmingham', shows the city in rather grim-looking silhouette.

Slumped on a sofa, Charlie is delighted to find his daily packet of Haribo Fun Mix – 'the King of sweets' – waiting, rips the packet open and dives in. 'It's vital to get the balance right in a packet of Haribo,' he muses. 'Obviously you need some of the foamy bits, but when there are too many fried eggs that's just overdoing it.' He produces a cola bottle from the bag and eyes it suspiciously. 'I once had a bag of Haribo and it was HALF COLA BOTTLES!' he shouts. 'WHAT AN ABSOLUTE SHOCKER!'

An innocuous-looking box has been placed on a coffee table. The lid opens to reveal a garishly decorated, home-made sponge cake which, a little investigation reveals, has been dropped off by fans as a gift for the band. James prods it suspiciously. 'Two years ago I would already be eating that cake,' James says as he continues to probe the sponge, 'but the things I've heard...'

What things?

'Things that you don't want to know. There could be *anything* in that cake. I once met a singer who took a huge mouthful of a cake they'd been baked by a fan, and suddenly realised that they had a mouthful of the fan's pubic hair.'

Why, we wonder, would anybody choose to bake their pubes into a cake? But James is already off. 'Pubic Cake – what a great name for a band. NO! What a great name for a single! It's our comeback single!' After a short pause, James changes his mind again: '*Pubic Cake* is the title of our American album.' Busted's American album is due out over the summer, and will combine the best bits from the band's first two LPs. Of course, it will be called nothing remotely like 'Pubic Cake', and as the tour progresses James will unveil an increasingly ludicrous series of title suggestions.

James maintains that 'Pubic Cake' is a good idea for a song. 'Send me Jaffa Cakes in a tube,' he sings, 'but don't send me a cake containing pubes.' James demands that Charlie improvises a tune on the guitar, but Charlie opts instead to strum Radiohead's 'Street Spirit (Fade Out)' as James attempts some more lyrics: 'I smell the pubes, they're in the pan cooking / And you thought I wasn't looking...'

ONE WORLD UNDER THE DOLLAR
SUBJUGATE
DEBASE

Matt has decided that a novel set piece would be to set himself on fire, to run around the stage and to be rescued from death by James with a fire extinguisher.

Thom Yorke, Matt speculates, would no doubt be extremely proud.

An hour later Charlie's strumming Blink-182's 'Miss You', and Matt is contemplating what to do after tonight's show. There are rumours of some sort of Playboy party in town. Before long, James's vocal warm-up exercises are audible from behind the closed toilet door. 'I'm wiping my bum, I'm wiping my bum, I'm wiping my bum,' he chimes, followed by a quick burst of 'Good King Wenceslas'. James, Matt says laughing, recently admitted that he used to indulge in boyband-style vocal ad-libs during hymns at school.

While they're waiting to go on stage, the boys are fitted with their microphone headsets. On the one hand these headsets are great – they allow the band to run around on stage rather than being rooted behind a static microphone stand. On the other hand, as James points out, they look ridiculous. 'I'm just *not* feeling like Michael Jackson,' he mopes as he pulls the set into position. 'I feel more like Garth Brooks.'

'Or,' Matt suggests, 'Steps.'

During tonight's gig Matt, who necks three Red Bulls immediately prior to appearing on stage, will invite the audience to pass judgement on the headsets. 'We do them differently from Garth Brooks and Steps,' he tells 11,000 fans. 'We make them cool, don't you think?' The audience's muted response speaks volumes, but Busted seem comfortable on stage tonight – James spots one 'I Love Busted' banner and tells its bearers that 'I love Busted too', while Charlie initiates what will become a running theme for subsequent shows by finding a pair of knickers, which have been thrown onto the stage, and putting them on Matt's head during the encore. 'Everyone laugh at Matt,' instructs Charlie.

'They're actually Charlie's pants,' Matt mutters.

The high spirits continue during our bus ride back to the hotel. We're talking about the show's pyrotechnics, and Matt has decided that a novel set piece would be to set himself on fire, run around the stage and be rescued from death by James with a fire extinguisher. This idea is quickly vetoed by Fletch, so other ideas are floated.

Charlie: Can I stagedive?

Fletch: I don't think that's a very good idea. Even if you managed to clear the six-foot camera pit, you'd be torn limb from limb.

Charlie: How ABOUT...How about I'm in a huge, see-through plastic ball? And I just...roll off the stage.

Matt: The fans could throw you around!

James: Fill it with helium!

In the hotel bar, drink flows once again. Some younger members of the entourage are on strict(ish) curfews and have been informed that they must be in bed by midnight, so they accelerate their boozing accordingly.

By 3 a.m. the bar is quietening down but, up in Room 420, the party continues. The entire corridor leading to Matt's room is thick with cigarette smoke; inside, one of Matt's musician mates is playing some of the tracks he's been working on back in London.

'You know,' Matt announces as the clock strikes four, 'I'm quite enjoying being on tour.'

March 6

Birmingham

'I suppose, hat or no hat, I did just get off the Busted tour bus.'

The next morning, we have arranged to meet Charlie in reception with the aim of going record shopping. First, though, it's time for breakfast, from the Subway sandwich bar over the road. Charlie disappears onto the tour bus in search of his disguise and, true to form, is recognised by fans within three seconds of clambering off the bus. 'I suppose, hat or no hat, I did just get off the Busted tour bus,' Charlie notes as he attempts to explain his disguise's most recent failure.

We cross the road to Subway, where Charlie buys a hot meatball Sub and promptly drops half of it down the front of a coat that is already caked in debris from other meals. Adam hops in a cab with us and we drive off in search of shops. The cabbie can recommend only one independent shop – Hard To Find Records – so we decide to first have a look at Birmingham's Bullring shopping centre, a huge mall whose outside is made of 15,000 silver discs and looks utterly insane. Adam agrees to meet us at the entrance half an hour later and we investigate the shopping centre, which includes a branch of Selfridges where Charlie is stopped and asked for an autograph, a MusicZone CD store where Charlie is stopped and asked for an autograph, and a Boots the chemist where Charlie is stopped and asked for an autograph.

In HMV, Charlie produces a CD from his inside pocket. 'Look at this,' he says. The CD is by a band called Bayside – Charlie had bought the CD in a London branch of HMV because the band are signed to his favourite record label, Victory Records, but when he got it home and removed the shrink-wrap there was no CD in the box. 'It was a bit of a shocker.' He explains his predicament to a guy behind the desk in HMV and the CD is exchanged. He takes the paper inlay card out and sniffs it. Charlie likes sniffing things made of paper.

We meet Adam outside – where, Charlie is horrified to discover, there are no benches. 'You can't beat a good bench for a nice sit down,' he exclaims in his typical, slightly eccentric fashion. 'But there are none here. What an absolute shocker.' (Many things will shock Charlie today.) Adam hails a cab, bundles Charlie into the back and agrees to meet him back at the hotel in a couple of hours. As Adam has learned in the past, when Charlie walks into a record shop he can be there for ages. We head off in the direction of Hard To Find Records, but when we get there it soon seems as if it might not be totally appropriate for Charlie's quest for unlistenable guitar music.

At one point a particularly miserable-looking Charlie finds himself trapped in the 1970s Disco section. 'I'm not sure about the "Hard To Find" factor,' he huffs. 'More like "Hard To Find Anything You Want".' He asks at the counter whether there are any other indie shops in Birmingham and is met with blank expressions. The shopping trip has been a disaster, and we wander back to the hotel.

On the way to the venue, Matt lies with his feet up on the seats and explains that his morning has been marginally more successful than Charlie's. While we were in comedy rave-music hell at Hard To Find, Matt had been clothes shopping in Selfridges. He came away with seven hats.

James announces that his solo song 'Loner In Love', which was dropped from a recent show due to a sore throat, will also be dropped from tonight's show for similar reasons, but cheers himself up by recounting the details of a car break-in his brother recently endured, in which the thieves took everything from the car except the Busted CDs.

The venue's dressing room has been tidied since yesterday, but the pubic cake remains in its box on the table. While Matt sets himself down for a session of PlayStation golf, James explains that last night, when he

NIKE
TOUR 04

'One of the first songs I learned was "Wonderwall", by Oasis.'

finally made it up to his hotel room, he had called up Tom from McFly for an impromptu songwriting session. The song they wrote will be called either 'Jen From The Fit Girls' Table' or 'The Girl From The Fit Girls' Table'. James reveals one of the secrets behind his songwriting. 'One of the first songs I learned was "Wonderwall" by Oasis,' he confides. 'And if you listen to them, you'll notice that a lot of our songs use the same technique as "Wonderwall". Noel Gallagher will probably hate that but it's his music that inspired us.'

It turns out that one of the doors in the corridor outside Busted's dressing room leads directly to the front-of-house ladies' toilet. Fortunately, for all sorts of reasons, the door is locked, but a five-millimetre gap underneath the door provides enough space for Matt to hold a conversation with a group of fans on the other side. After five minutes of winding the fans up, he rummages around in his bag and pulls out a bag of red chewy-bootlace sweets.

'Don't eat those,' comes a voice from outside the room. Once again it is Holly Day. 'They'll give you constipation.' Holly seems to know a lot about constipation.

Matt looks a little put out. 'I got them from Ikea,' he pleads, as if the act of buying sweets from a Swedish furniture warehouse somehow makes them fit for consumption. 'In fact, they're the best thing about Ikea.' He stuffs a handful in his mouth.

Half an hour before Busted are due on stage, the band are discussing musical influences with Fletch and assorted members of the touring crew. 'Of course,' James announces, 'Charlie's main musical influence is Chad Kroeger from Nickelback.'

Nickelback are rightly regarded as one of the very worst rock acts on the face of Planet Earth and this slur – vindictive by anyone's standards – throws Charlie into such a rage that he grabs a bottle of water from the rider and hurls it across the room. It bounces on the floor and hits James in the leg, prompting James to throw himself on the floor, bleating something about an injury. This sort of display is so routine in the Busted family that nobody takes much notice, which just makes James howl ever louder, and five minutes later he is still clutching his leg. 'Seriously guys,' he begs, 'it really hurts.'

Fletch and Richard Rashman exchange worried glances. There are, Fletch will later explain, two possibilities here: that James actually had hurt his leg, which seems unlikely as nobody actually saw the bottle make contact, or that James was making a song and dance out of nothing and the joke went too far. Either way, by the time James is propelled up through the stage at the beginning of 'Air Hostess', his injuries seem to have been forgotten.

It's another good show – at one point Matt jumps so hard that he breaks one of the steps on the stage

– and the band's between-song banter is coming on in leaps and bounds. So much so that, when Charlie announces, as he has every night, that 'There comes a time in every show where we have to say goodnight', Matt butts in.

'Actually,' he begins, 'this isn't going to be our last song at all. We're going to go off stage, have a drink of water and a sit down for three minutes, and then we're going to come back on and play some more songs. It's called an encore, and I've just ruined it.'

Back at the hotel bar, Matt's still having trouble coming to terms with how many fans are out there in the audience each night. 'I can't fathom it,' he says, and a look of horror spreads across his face. '*Fathom*? What kind of person says "fathom"? I've been hanging around with Charlie for too long.'

At 3.15 a.m., after an unexplained absence, James reappears with an acoustic guitar and announces that the stragglers are to write a song, here and now. Many people are wearing hats: of the seven caps he bought on this morning's shopping spree, Matt has so far given away five.

March 7

Shef-field

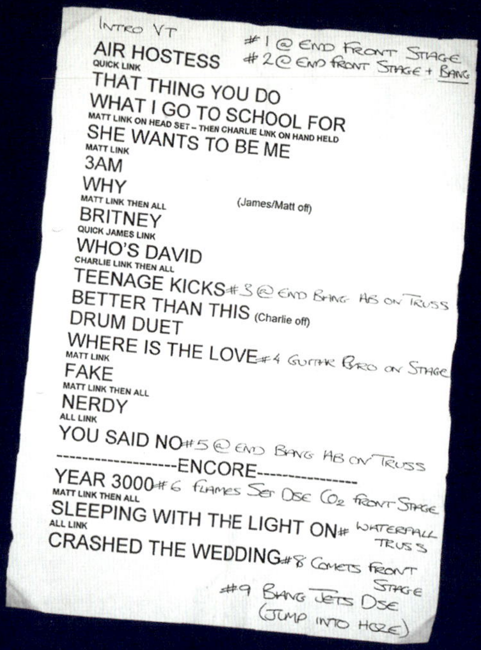

INTRO VT

AIR HOSTESS #1 @ END FRONT STAGE #2 @ END FRONT STAGE + BANG

QUICK LINK

THAT THING YOU DO

WHAT I GO TO SCHOOL FOR

MATT LINK ON HEAD SET – THEN CHARLIE LINK ON HAND HELD

SHE WANTS TO BE ME

MATT LINK

3AM

WHY

MATT LINK THEN ALL (James/Matt off)

BRITNEY

QUICK JAMES LINK

WHO'S DAVID

CHARLIE LINK THEN ALL

TEENAGE KICKS #3 @ END BANG HB ON TRUSS

BETTER THAN THIS (Charlie off)

DRUM DUET

WHERE IS THE LOVE #4 GUITAR PYRO ON STAGE

MATT LINK

FAKE

MATT LINK THEN ALL

NERDY

ALL LINK

YOU SAID NO #5 @ END BANG HB ON TRUSS

-------------------ENCORE-----------------

YEAR 3000 #6 FLAMES SET DSE CO2 FRONT STAGE

MATT LINK THEN ALL

SLEEPING WITH THE LIGHT ON # WATERFALL TRUSS

ALL LINK

CRASHED THE WEDDING #8 COMETS FRONT STAGE

#9 BANG JETS DSE (JUMP INTO HOZE)

Although we've stayed the night in Birmingham, and will stay here once again this evening, today's show is in Sheffield, which is around an hour and a half away by tour bus. When we arrive, Sheffield Arena doesn't seem as plush as Birmingham. The main seating area of the arena appears to have been covered with chipboard and the band's dressing room is tiny. The rest of the entourage's dressing rooms are three times as big, but nobody tells Matt, James and Charlie – this is one of those things the boys are best discovering for themselves.

In the Busted dressing room, James is struggling with a T-shirt. 'My T-shirt's too tight,' he eventually decides. 'I need a new one.'

'Or,' Richard Rashman murmurs from behind a newspaper, 'a diet.'

One of the topics open for discussion over the past few days has been the tour set list, and whether the band have misjudged demand for songs from the first album. In particular it is felt that songs like 'Dawson's Geek' or 'Britney' could help some audiences feel more familiar with the show, since some fans might not be well acquainted with *A Present For Everyone* and, with the exception of the band's first four singles, there's nothing in the show from the *Busted* album. Support for the addition of 'Britney' seems particularly strong, since Britney's new single 'Toxic' is on course to hit Number One in this Sunday's chart, meaning that the star is once again as popular as she was when James first wrote the song four years ago.

'I think we should leave the set list as it is.' Charlie shrugs. 'We're touring the second album, we're really proud of the second album, we're having a brilliant time on stage each night performing it, and the audience are loving it too. Why change?'

'There's some feeling at the record label that an older song wouldn't do any harm,' suggests Fletch.

'But,' Charlie responds, 'this isn't the *A Ticket For Everyone At The Record Label* tour. It's the *A Ticket For EVERYONE* tour.'

Someone wonders out loud whether Fletch might be right, at least in the sense that there seems to be a bit of a 'dip' in the show as it stands.

'Well obviously,' James mugs, 'there's a massive dip where "Loner In Love" should be. People are running from the arenas crying because they haven't seen me perform my solo song.'

Before long Charlie has lost interest in the conversation and is grappling with a racing game on the PlayStation. 'Get ready,' he warns, 'for a dangerous game of...of...' There is a long pause. 'Of thought!'

Outside a group of fans have gathered by the large fence marking out the backstage car park, and Busted decide to go and sign some autographs. Almost as soon as they arrive outside it begins to rain which, combined with the wire fence, makes the whole scene rather a lot like the tATu 'All The Things She Said' video, except without the Russians or the lesbian angle.

Three of the girls explain that they recently grouped together and entered a local talent show as Busted (they won); another fan has crafted an elaborate black banner with the word 'MATT' spelled out in hundreds of flashing fairy lights. One fan, Gemma, has been waiting for three days to meet the boys. She went to both Birmingham shows and has been here at Sheffield since midday. She says that, while she does live nearby, she spends a lot of time hanging around, waiting to meet bands. 'So far,' she declares, 'I have met Westlife, Blue, D-Side, Phixx, Triple 8, Mark Owen, Darius, Sugababes and A1.' She explains that coming to this sort of thing isn't all about meeting the band – on many occasions that simply won't happen, and sometimes it's just nice to catch up with other fans. 'It's

a chance to say really stupid obsessive stuff that non-fans don't appreciate,' she says with a grin.

Amid the scrum, Gemma has managed to get her album sleeve signed by Matt. 'James signed for the people next to me then ran off,' she moans, 'and Charlie totally cut around the corner I was standing at. Still, I'd not got Matt's autograph before, so I'm quite happy about that.'

Busted share a table with McFly for dinner as Matt flicks through a copy of the *NME* and Charlie tucks into tonight's food – Scotch broth for the starter, turkey with various (but not quite all the) trimmings for the main course, rice pudding for dessert. Straight after his last mouthful of rice pudding Charlie announces that he is exhausted and disappears for half an hour's sleep on the tour bus.

Later on, in the stuffy, claustrophobic dressing room, Matt looks round at James (head back on the sofa, staring silently at the ceiling) and Charlie (back from his sleep and idly plucking away at an acoustic guitar) and looks momentarily concerned. 'I don't think we're the same energetic Busted we once were,' he says. 'We need to get our energy back.'

To wake himself up before the gig, Matt runs off to the tour bus to retrieve the band football. With a degree of inevitability it is only a matter of minutes before he's sprawled on a couch clutching his leg, having hoofed the ball down the corridor and somehow injured himself. There are 45 minutes left until the band are due on stage – giving Neil, the band's resident physiotherapist, a little longer to work his magic than he had yesterday with the James/Evian bottle farrago. Before long, Matt's knee is bandaged up for support and being soothed with an emergency ice pack, but his limp won't make for much in the way of showmanship when he takes to the stage.

For the first few songs of tonight's show, things certainly aren't looking good, and after fifteen minutes Fletch leaves his regular position at the sound desk – where he's been for the duration of every show so far – and makes his way back to the dressing room. A few minutes later, during Matt and James's performance of 'Better Than This', Charlie has seized his opportunity for a toilet break and bursts into the dressing room to use the bathroom. To his surprise, he finds Fletch sat on the sofa.

'Hi, Fletch,' he says, as he undoes his flies.

'Hello, Charlie.'

'What are you doing in here?'

'I'm really disappointed in tonight's show. I know you can do so much better and I just can't bear to watch tonight, mate. Sorry.'

Five minutes after Charlie has bounded back out of the bathroom, Fletch's curiosity gets the better of him, and he decides to watch what remains of the show. In fairness, it's far better than anyone would expect from a band with two injured members. Matt has become so swept away once again in the thrill of performing for 11,000 people that he somehow forgets his injury and gives it his all; even James, whose leg is still purportedly injured from the Evian Incident, puts in a great performance.

Waiting on the bus after the show, Charlie decides to clamber into the driving seat. Given that on receipt of his Porsche last spring he managed to collide with another vehicle within one week, some worried glances are exchanged in the lounge area, especially when Charlie leans back and asks, 'Is this like driving a car then? Where are the keys?'

On the way back to the hotel, we bring up Matt's earlier comment about Busted's waning energy. Some nights, watching McFly tearing around the stage has thrown Busted's 2004 stage

'So,' begins the police constable with his notebook open, 'can one of you tell me exactly what happened?'

presence into even sharper contrast with the perky, fun-filled Busted of the 'What I Go To School For' era.

'I think that's good in a way,' Charlie announces. 'The further we go away from that the better. We're still energetic, we're just not so happy-clappy.'

'I didn't like tonight's show,' James suddenly says.

'It was great tonight,' Matt counters. 'Partly because there were loads of teenage blokes in the audience. I was looking at them thinking, I bet you lot pretend not to like Busted at college – but I know you bloody love us!'

As the long journey drags on, Charlie and James disappear upstairs for a game of Connect 4 while Matt, Fletch, physio Neil and James's brother Nick stay downstairs and watch *Phoenix Nights* on DVD. After what seems like an age, we arrive back at the hotel. Three days of late nights and hard work have taken their toll on most of the crew. The hotel bar is empty.

'Let's just have a quiet drink in the bar and go to bed,' Matt suggests.

Four hours later the intermittent flashing blue light of a parked police car illuminates the hotel bar. 'So,' begins the police officer with his notebook open, 'can one of you

tell me exactly what happened?'

'Well,' Matt begins. 'The idea was to have a quiet drink and then go to bed...'

But that's not exactly what happened. Flashback four hours: after the one quiet drink it strikes James and Matt that, with a day off from touring tomorrow, there is no real reason for the drinks to stop at one, or two; or even for those drinks to be particularly quiet.

The booze begins to escalate from pints of lager to shots of tequila and before long Matt is behind the hotel bar, harassing a member of the night staff. 'Where are your spirits?' Matt demands. 'Do you do Aftershock?' (Matt is referring to the bright red, syrupy booze only ever consumed by people who are already drunk.) 'Let me give you a hand. Where are your cigars?'

A short while later, having decided that the miraculous healing power of alcohol has cured his dodgy leg, Matt has found a pair of scissors and cut off the bandage on his knee. It lies in the ashtray.

As it becomes increasingly obvious that the night porter – who bears no resemblance whatsoever to a 70s cowboy-movie star but has been christened Clint Eastwood by Matt and James – is hoping to close the bar, we move up to Matt's bedroom, Room 420. A call to Clint Eastwood produces a tray bearing three pints of Stella and three double JD & Cokes, one of which is promptly spilled on the floor as Matt swings around brandishing one of the two remaining baseball caps from yesterday's hat spree. 'I'm going to distress it,' he announces, and sets about the peak with a pair of scissors. The finished item looks less like a customised fashion accessory than a £16.99 cap whose peak has been cut up by a pissed-up member of Busted, but Matt seems pleased with his handiwork and pulls the cap onto his head.

The window has been left open by the maid responsible for today's room service and before long the contents of Matt's fruit basket – two bananas and a handful of grapes – have been thrown from our fourth-floor location onto the street below. The room's litter bin is the next item

to go sailing through the night air. Matt and James pull back from the window and take a look around the room. Matt has not yet finished with the window.

In the corner of the room is a large wooden cabinet, and in it is a 24-inch hotel TV. Hotel televisions are massive things that don't work like proper televisions. They spring to life for no reason, informing you that someone's silver Lexus is blocking traffic in the car park and could it please be moved before it is towed away; they have secret late-night channels showing films of people kissing each other, and they are fine-tuned to show nothing else that anybody would really want to watch. This particular hotel television, Matt jokes, is going out of the window.

After reaching round both sides of the set and pulling it out of the shelf – and out of the plug socket – Matt staggers around the room, then heads over to the window. When he walks back into the centre of the room, he is sans television. Two seconds later, we hear a huge smash.

James looks rather surprised. He will later explain that until Matt returned from the window – looking a little surprised himself – it had looked like he was just having a laugh. We all peer from the hotel window. There's a lot of glass, plastic and circuitry lining the pavement.

It is, we all decide, time to go for a walk. As we head for the revolving doors on the way out of the hotel, the following exchange takes place.

Concierge: Have you just thrown a television out of your window?

Matt: No.

Concierge: All right then.

It's now 4 a.m. and we're wandering the streets of Birmingham. Through an underpass, past a strand of shops. We turn right, down Ryland Street, and then right again, into Rosel Way. It's a dead end. We turn back, then right again, into another dead end. By 4.20 we're lost, and Matt is on the ground following an ill-advised piggyback. We walk for a while longer until at 4.45 a.m. James spots a landmark ahead of us: the remains of a TV set, splashed across the pavement. It seems we've found the hotel, but, as we turn the corner into the hotel car park, we also find a police car.

Fletch and Adam are in reception talking to a policeman.

'So,' begins the police constable with his notebook open, 'can one of you tell me exactly what happened?'

The thrust of Matt's defence is this: 'I was really drunk, I thought I was being funny, and then it got out of hand and I was really stupid.'

In the cold light of a hotel bar at 5 a.m. on a Monday, it's difficult not to agree. The police officer walks back out to reception to discuss what has happened with the hotel manager. In situations like this, further action is at the discretion of the hotel and the police officer in question. Between them they decide not to take matters any further, but that doesn't stop them giving Matt a bit of a scare.

'Well, Mr Willis,' the policeman says as he comes back into the bar, 'I'm afraid I'm going to have to ask you to sign a confession.'

Matt looks gutted and then quite surprised when the 'form' placed in front of him is just a blank sheet of paper. And that, apart from a few sheepish glances exchanged between James, Matt and whichever idiot had been complaining in Matt's hotel room that his on-the-road book needed some excitement, is that.

Now it really is time for bed.

March 9

Car-diff

'Every time I walked in they were playing another song – "Year 3000", "What I Go To School For", whatever. When Charlie joined the band I knew it was going to be amazing.'

It does not take long for the details of Matt's brush with the law to make their way into the *Sun* newspaper. Under the headline 'Busted Chuck Toaster Out Of Hotel Window', the paper's showbiz correspondent Victoria Newton writes:

BUSTED are doing their best to prove they're not a squeaky-clean pop band – by chucking stuff out of hotel windows. Matt caused £1,500 worth of damage at Birmingham's plush Marriott Hotel when he hurled...Yes, you've guessed it...a TV out of the window in the early hours of Monday. Very rock'n'roll. But the lads proved they are newcomers to hell-raising by opening the window ***first*** *rather than throwing the telly through the glass – and then truly embarrassed themselves by then tossing out a toaster.* ***A toaster?*** *Drum kits and TVs maybe, boys — but not kitchen appliances. They're so, well, domestic.*

Now the dust has settled, Matt is suitably mortified, and still has a massive black-and-purple bruise on his right hip from the après-TV piggybacking incident.

In the dressing room Charlie, the only member of the band to have been safely tucked up in bed when the TV was introduced to that Birmingham pavement, recalls hearing the news for the first time. 'I was really shocked when I heard,' he admits. 'I thought it would end up looking really stupid – that people who didn't like Busted were going to have a field day with it. I guess I was right in a way, but I'm not pissed off with Matt.'

Would you ever throw a TV out of a window?

'I wouldn't say that I'd *never* throw a TV out of a window, but I'd never do it quite like that. I find a lot of things about "rock and roll" quite clichéd.'

Charlie dismisses the incident as an example of how easy it is to get restless on tour, and it's hard not to see his point. Days merge into each other in an endless blur of dressing rooms, soundchecks, snoozes on the tour bus and meals in catering. 'I'm the kind of person who gets bored very easily,' Charlie admits, 'but being on the road at least means that you're moving around all the time, and it's not really a hard life getting up at one, doing a gig and then having a drink afterwards.' He considers his words. 'Actually, I think "bored" is totally the wrong word, but there's a lot of hanging around. It's more a case of being frustrated, of wanting to go off and actually *do* something.'

Watching tonight's show is James's younger brother Nick, who joined the tour a few days ago and intends to stay on for as long as possible until someone chucks him off the bus. 'James just said to me, "Come along",' he reasons, 'so here I am.' In a way, Nick knows more about the early days of Busted than anyone outside the band. He remembers the day back at his and James's parents' Southend house when, all of a sudden, Matt turned up to stay. 'They'd spend all their time downstairs round the piano, just writing songs,' Nick remembers. 'Every time I walked in they were playing another song – "Year 3000", "What I Go To School For", whatever. When Charlie joined the band I knew it was going to be amazing. He just made it, really.'

Nick remembers Matt as the perfect house guest – 'When he finished dinner he took his plate to the sink' – and recalls that on the day of his GCSE results he was generously rewarded by Matt. 'He had a massive party for me in my house. He poured loads of different things in a jug and we drank it. The first time I ever got drunk was with Matt.'

After the show Matt is moaning about his hotel room ('It's not as big as Prince Charles's room,' he says, laughing and prodding Charlie in the back) and chatting with Fletch's family, who've come along for a few of the dates. Some of Charlie's friends from Uppingham have also joined us in the bar, but, with another gig tomorrow and the exhausting tour lifestyle kicking in, it's not long before everyone calls it a night and heads to bed.

ENTRANCE
NEXT DOOR

‘I’d really, really love to collaborate with the guy who wrote the *Teenage Mutant Ninja Turtles* theme.’

March 10

Car-diff

Over breakfast, James mentions the theme tune he submitted one year ago for a new animated MTV show called *Smart Alecs*. He sings it for the benefit of those assembled in the hotel breakfast room, even though he won't sing it on the show. Until last week, he explains, he'd forgotten all about the song, but has just heard that it will definitely be used on the show. 'I'd really, really love to collaborate with the guy who wrote the *Teenage Mutant Ninja Turtles* theme,' he announces. 'That was such a clever song.'

At the venue James takes receipt of an advance copy of the debut solo album by *NSYNC star JC Chasez. He slips it into the stereo and flicks through the tracks, deconstructing each one and judging most on how much they sound like Michael Jackson. One song, a high-energy electro thumper, boasts a chorus in which JC yells 'ALL DAY LONG I DREAM ABOUT SEX!' over and over again. It splits dressing-room opinion. James thinks it's funny. Matt says he could imagine dancing to it when pissed. Charlie, to nobody's surprise, denounces it as 'bloody awful' and decides that it's time to visit catering.

On returning to the dressing room we find the place strewn with presents from fans. Among them is a blue gift bag containing a DVD of the Clash (one of Matt's favourite bands) and a glossy biography of punk icon Sid Vicious, as well as two badges ('Mine's A Pint' and 'Beer Monster') and a key ring bearing the words 'Pissed and happy'. 'I feel so guilty,' Matt says. 'Someone's gone to all this bother and spent so much money, but I've already got the Sid Vicious book.'

Well, at least, someone points out, that means they got you something you wanted, in a way.

'Well, yeah, I suppose.' He flicks through the book. It makes for grim reading: Sid died when he was young after years of horrible drug abuse and self-mutilation, all well accounted in the pictures flicking before Matt's eyes – a wasted life on fast-forward, heading for oblivion. 'What a waste,' Matt whispers under his breath, almost inaudibly. 'What a bloody waste.'

James recalls one set of gifts he received from a fan last year. 'He got me some signed photos of Michael Jackson and Michael J Fox, and I did ask him, "Are these real?" He said yes. It seemed a bit rude to ask any more because they were a gift, but I'm quite good at forging signatures myself and I had a look at them later on and the Michaels were the same on both autographs. It was a nice thought, though.'

He mentions his slight regret at claiming, in an early Busted interview, that he was addicted to Jaffa Cakes. 'At one record signing a few months later everyone who came had bought me a box of Jaffa Cakes – I went away with three bin liners full of them. I still like Jaffa Cakes but, as you can imagine, I've got cupboards full of them at home. Still, they do come in useful when I'm peckish.'

March 12

London

'My regret is that we haven't partied hard enough or got off with enough girls. We intend to sort that out tonight.'

It's only 2 p.m. but at Wembley Arena tour manager Adam is already busy. 'I always dread coming to Wembley,' he says. 'It wouldn't be so bad but because the entire music industry is based here in London it's not long before you start getting the phone calls: "My next-door neighbour's kid is a really big fan"; "Someone I once met in Tesco's brother's daughter once walked past someone in the street whose pet dog loves Charlie"...'

Wembley's backstage area isn't as big as the other venues we've been in so far – there's just room for a small walkway between the back gates and the ramps which lead to the stage, and at opposite sides of the backstage area are, on the left, Woody's Bar (which is where the meet-and-greets take place before the gig, and boozing will occur afterwards) and, on the right, The Clifford, which is where catering can be found. Busted's own dressing room seems the most well decorated of all those lining the corridors – with floorboards and green leather seating – but even the mirrored walls don't disguise the fact that this 'Elvin Suite' seems the smallest of the lot.

Walking around the empty arena brings back memories for keyboardist Chris Banks. Once upon a time a rather younger Chris worked here at Wembley, getting paid £3.60 per hour to wander around the audience flogging tour programmes. All went well until one fateful weekend when he dumped his programmes, found an empty seat and sat down to watch Michael Jackson two nights in a row. He was relieved of his job shortly afterwards and so, he says, it's nice to return now, and to finally be on stage.

As a group of current Wembley employees wrestle with the metal crash barriers, the band bang their way through a soundcheck. The 'Loner In Love' saga has now finally been concluded and 'Britney' has been added to the set list in its place. It sounds great live, but it wasn't included in the original sessions at John Henry's rehearsal studio back in February so it's important that the band seize soundcheck time to brush up on the song, since they haven't performed it much since last spring's UK theatre tour.

James is philosophical about his moment of solo glory being axed. 'I loved doing the song at the Irish dates,' he says, 'but it got to the point where I couldn't do it because of my voice, and the show worked all right without it. Also, you can only do what you want to a certain extent and the fans who've bought the tickets would probably prefer "Britney". I sing a lot of "Britney" anyway. It's no big deal.'

The first of today's official duties is an interview for a local London radio station. James, Matt and Charlie huddle by the side of the stage as the interviewer talks them through what will happen – they'll add in a load of crowd noise back at the station, making it sound as if Busted are just about to go on stage.

Interviewer: Do you have any regrets about the tour?

James: No regrets. They don't work, and they only hurt.

Matt: My regret is that we haven't partied hard enough or got off with enough girls. We intend to sort that out tonight.

Interviewer (now on the tour bus): What's in your fridge?

James (actually on the tour bus rather than pretending to be): The remains of a Malteser Easter egg, and some beer.

Interviewer: Do you have any gossip about any other pop stars?

James: Yes. (Name withheld) is pregnant.

Matt: JAMES! You can't say that! It's not true!

James: How do you know it's not true?

Matt:...

James: *Well* then.

The interview soon degenerates, but the radio people seem happy with what they've got and the 'stop' button is pressed, signalling that it is time for the boys to visit catering.

Charlie reads this week's copy of London listings magazine *Time Out* and seems pleased with the cover feature, an interview with Busted about the band's past, present and future. In particular, it addresses the persistent rumours that he is to quit Busted. These rumours have been circulating since before Christmas. 'It's a sensitive issue which is a bit like stepping on glass,' Charlie warns this afternoon. 'Actually, not just glass – CRACKED glass!'

Before Christmas, didn't it seem that there were new rumours every day that he was to leave the band?

'Yes.' He nods. 'It was "Charlie's leaving Busted" all the time.'

Were you leaving Busted?

'No. I was never leaving Busted. But what was happening was that I was getting my other band, Fight Star, together, and nobody seemed quite sure where that left Busted. In the sense that I didn't know if people were behind me, and I think at the same time they might have thought that I wasn't committed to Busted any more.'

How did you sort it out?

'I had two long chats with Richard and Fletch. What frustrated me wasn't that I didn't like Busted, or that I didn't want to be in Busted. It was the fact that I didn't feel like what I wanted to do with Fight Star was being taken seriously. I was like, "This is really important for me, and I need to be happy about it to make it work." And they were like, "Oh, all right. Well that's fine then. If your heart's in it, so is ours."'

Was it really sorted out just like that?

'Yeah. One thing I learned from that was how important it is to discuss things really early on, before they have a chance to get out of hand. Ironically, the whole thing had been sorted out before the "Charlie's leaving" stories even started in the press, so by the time they were printed it was all over.'

With that out of the way, is there anything else that would end Busted?

'That was the only problem we've ever had, and looking back now it wasn't even a big deal. I wasn't happy about something, we talked about it, it was sorted out. It was a storm in a teacup. As long as I don't feel I'm having the wool pulled over the eyes just to make me happy, it'll be fine.'

How are Fight Star doing now?

'We're going great. Now it's just a case of doing some more gigs. Our first proper gig has gone on sale and without any promotion it's sold twenty tickets at the Barfly club in London. I'm really excited.'

Isn't it funny that you should be sitting here backstage at one of six sold-out nights at an 11,000-capacity arena, and that you should be just as excited about selling twenty tickets for a tiny Camden show?

'They're full-price tickets, you know. For people to actually ring up and do the business with their credit cards, just for Fight Star, is awesome.'

What's full price?

'Seven pounds fifty. Plus booking fee.'

The boys make the final amendments to their personal guest lists – Matt has an astonishing nineteen people coming to see him tonight and, being Matt's mates, they'll all require access to the bar afterwards – and upstairs, in the public corridors surrounding the arena, the Wembley Arena staff are out in force selling candy floss, popcorn, hot dogs and massive tubs of Maltesers. You can taste the sweetness in the air. 'What's wrong with a nice salad?' mutters one beleaguered parent.

Spoiled for choice by bands who

March 12

The atmosphere before Busted go on stage tonight is one of the most electric of the tour so far.

always put London on their schedules, audiences in the capital are notoriously difficult to impress, but the atmosphere before Busted go on stage tonight is one of the most electric of the tour so far. The whole arena is dotted with small reminders of the acts who've appeared here in the past. In the main entrance there is a poster from the first *Fame Academy* tour, signed by the performers – David Sneddon, Sinead Quinn, Ainslie Henderson, and seven others. With the exception of Lemar, every single one of those singers has been dropped. In Woody's Bar, Matt's checking out a gallery of photographs, all taken of bands when they played at Wembley Arena. The Rolling Stones, Alice Cooper, Rod Stewart, Kylie Minogue. 'No room for Hear'say,' he hoots.

Busted's press officer, Heather Redmond, is bustling around backstage sorting out tickets for the journalists who'll be reviewing tonight's show. Twenty minutes before the band are due on stage we're also joined by a group of world-weary photographers, herded in here so they don't get up to any mischief before they're led out to the photo pit.

When the band finally take to the stage Charlie manages to get his 'Hello, Wembley!' in first; Matt is speechless, eventually mustering an 'Outrageous' as the Busted fans' screaming is somehow drowned out by the intermittent chants of 'RUDE BOY! RUDE BOY!' from Matt's nineteen mates. The recent change in the set list makes for some great moments on stage, like this one:

James: Is there anyone out there called David? (Audience goes bonkers.) Wow, there are a lot of girls out there called David. What kind of a parent calls their baby girl David? So do you know a guy called David? He's gonna screw you over. This one's 'Who's David'...

Charlie: Actually, we're gonna play 'Britney'.

James: All right then, we're gonna play 'Britney' now, just because *Charlie* wants to...

In the dressing room afterwards, concert promoter Simon Moran appears with bottles of champagne and the boys toast their first ever Wembley date.

Premier

March 13

London

'Look at that! Look at all those people! Look at all those people COMING TO MY CONCERT!'

Busted find a discarded banner from last night's show and examine the handiwork. Across it is written, 'Remember us from holiday?'

'You know what?' James says, 'I think I actually *do* remember them from holiday.'

At 2 p.m., Matt has already confirmed his boredom and persuades the tour's head of security, Barry Knight, to take him to the nearby branch of Blockbuster in order to stock up on DVDs and PlayStation games. Matt hops into the front passenger seat of Barry's people carrier – normally used to transport Damon and the two Chrises, and bearing the stains to prove it – and we drive through the massive backstage gates. Matt winds his window down and some girls scream at him. He spends the rest of the five-minute journey with his head hanging out of the window, rather like dogs have a habit of doing. It's worth pointing out, however, that dogs rarely scream, 'Look at that! Look at all those people! Look at all those people COMING TO MY CONCERT!'

When we arrive at Blockbuster Matt makes a beeline for the *Bad Boys II* DVD and, after some serious thought, picks out three games worthy of taking back to the dressing room. At the checkout, Matt points at a table full of dodgy DVDs. 'Which of those would be the one you wouldn't dream of watching in a million years?' he asks. We plump for something called *Kangaroo Jack*, whose 80s-style box bears a picture of a kangaroo wearing sunglasses.

'Exactly. And yet I saw it the other day and it was really good. You cannot,' Matt concludes, 'judge a DVD by its cover.'

On the way back, Matt says hello to fans from out of the window and wonders what would happen if he got out of the car and walked back alone. 'Chaos.' Barry laughs. He remembers the time in the 80s when he worked with a band called Bros (three-piece pop sensation, played their own instruments, etc.). At the height of their fame Matt Goss, the singer from the band, spotted a kid in a school playground wearing a denim jacket with a picture of his face on the back. He shot out of the car, jumped over the school fence, sprinted up to the boy and tapped him on the shoulder. He said hello, and then ran back, over the fence, into the car and they sped off. The whole episode was over in less than thirty seconds, but the pandemonium in the school playground would last for hours. 'I might do that tomorrow, then,' Matt decides.

Back at the arena, the audience begin to filter in just after 6 p.m. Each night on the Busted tour – and on every other big arena tour – they play pop videos and advertisements for ringtones on the big screens. They also play montages in which short clips of various pop stars are set to music. For the audience, there are very strict rules to follow during these montages.

1. If the people flashing up are responsible for your evening's entertainment (e.g. they are Busted, the punk-pop trio whose unique sound has revolutionised the British pop scene etc. etc. etc.), go absolutely bonkers

2. If the people flashing up are boys who are not responsible for your evening's entertainment, shout a bit but don't overdo it because that would frankly just be rude

3. If a girl's face pops up, look bored and shuffle your feet...

4. ...unless it's Kylie, or Cheryl from Girls Aloud, in which case you're allowed to whoop a little bit

5. And there we have it

What's interesting about these montages – which are identical each night – is how differently audiences will respond around the country: to Justin Timberlake (huge response in Sheffield, more muted in Cardiff), to Blue (big in London, not so big in Manchester), and so on. After tonight's gig we point out to Charlie that this clearly means something terribly important about the socio-geographic mapping of UK pop consumption. 'The screaming hurts my ears,' he says.

March 14

London

It is Sunday, and none of Busted have been to church.

There's plenty of work to do today. First off is an interview with another Spanish pop magazine. Mary Bell, the marketing manager for Universal Spain, is here to explain to the lads what's what with the whole Busted-being-popular-in-Spain thing. 'Crashed The Wedding', she says, is currently at Number 6 in the Spanish pop charts, and *A Present For Everyone* is due for release any week now.

'That's awesome,' says Matt. 'We haven't even *been* there!'

'I know,' Mary Bell replies, with a you'd-be-higher-than-Number-6-if-you-had-been smile.

It's time for the first interview, with the brilliantly named *SuperPop* magazine.

Superpop: Can you describe your sound?

Charlie: It's pop music, with guitars.

Superpop: Pop rock?

Charlie: It *was* pop rock. Now it's rock pop.

Superpop: What's it like being famous?

Matt: It's very weird. It's a bit like looking in on someone else being famous, from the outside.

Superpop: What will you be like in the future?

James: Like this, but with beards.

Matt: And pubes. I really hope that, by this time next year, we have pubes. Maybe I'd like a dog and a Range Rover too. And we'll all meet up every three weeks. And in the year 2025 we're going to meet up every two years and tour the world.

James: I'd like to do a Caribbean tour.

Superpop: Do you like Caribbean music?

James: No.

After the interview has finished I ask Charlie, who sometimes seems the most distracted in interviews, how he'd conduct things if he'd been sent off to interview Busted himself.

'I'd ask them why they thought they weren't taken as seriously as they'd like to be, by the serious press,' he replies.

But you know why that is.

'Yes.'

What would your answer be, then?

'My answer would be that I don't think people like to accept the fact that pop music can have anything good about it. Because pop music has been so bad for so long that it's difficult to remember or imagine a time when it was or could be amazing.'

Don't you think that the reason the serious, adult press have a problem with Busted is because you're marketed at children?

'It is. And people can't see past that. I find it very difficult myself sometimes to see through marketing, but there is something here with Busted that is good, that even the marketing can't obscure. Look how many adults you see on the tube reading *Harry Potter*.'

One of the alterations made to tonight's set will be the appearance of *Top Of The Pops* Saturday presenter, Fearne Cotton. During the Busted soundcheck she rehearses her bit, too – coming on between songs with a cameraman and sound guy, and introducing 'She Wants To Be Me' from the stage. She'll do it again for real in tonight's show.

Outside, two members of the Wembley security team discuss whether beige or red uniforms are best.

'You look more official in red,' muses one.

'Beige is a bit less angry though,' says the other.

'Yes,' says the first. 'It's good to be less angry.'

During the early stages of tonight's show, Busted have a guest on stage

'There is something here with Busted that is good, that even the marketing can't obscure. Look how many adults you see on the Tube reading *Harry Potter*.'

– and it's not Fearne Cotton. In the final verse of 'Air Hostess', a guy with unfortunate bleached hair, who looks about seventeen or eighteen, somehow manages to jump over the security fence at the front of the stage and then – rather impressively, on reflection – scale the six-foot stage. It all happens so quickly that nobody is on stage to remove him, so it's fortunate that, like many stage invaders, the hapless boy doesn't prove a serious threat and realises only when he's in front of 11,000 people that he hasn't got a clue what to do next. He stands there for a second and waves his hands at the crowd, then sees Barry Knight looming into view and darts up one of the runways. He weaves around Barry's grasping hands and runs back down to the front, where he is eventually caught and dragged off. The whole escapade lasts for less than twenty seconds. 'You could have got your head blown off!' Barry yells at the guy, and points to the stage. Two seconds later 'Air Hostess' finishes and a massive pyrotechnic explodes at the front of the stage, right where the luckless trespasser had clambered up.

While Matt begins his solo spot for 'Better Than This' – for which he is joined by hit songwriter Guy Chambers, replacing James on guitar for this song – one group of fans are making enough noise for their entire block. Irene, Louise, Melissa, Helen, Kate and Grace – all seventeen – have made their way from Surrey today on a shambolic journey including wrong tube stops, late trains, broken-down buses and an eager busker who agreed to play 'Sleeping With The Light On' on the London underground. 'We've been fans right from the beginning,' says Irene, 'and we got our tickets the first day they went on sale...' She begins to say something else, but then Matt sprints to our side of the stage and she goes back to screaming her head off.

This being the final Wembley night before the band head to Glasgow, the equipment is being packed up backstage before the encore has even started. Tomorrow it will begin its journey to Glasgow, and will be set up all over again.

March 16

Glasgow

Matt drifts in and out of sleep on the Busted tour bus. As he snoozes, James comments on Matt's more-than-passing resemblance to one of the Oompa-Loompas from *Charlie And The Chocolate Factory*. The conversation turns to the forthcoming Hollywood remake of the film and then, oddly, to James's friend Paul. Paul, it emerges, is a dwarf stuntman. Now awake, Matt is informed by Charlie of the Oompa-Loompa suggestion. 'So I am a short fat orange dwarf, with green hair,' he muses. 'I don't like the implication there...I'm not sure what the implication might be, but I'm sure I don't like it.'

Matt falls asleep once more, while James announces with a flourish that he has decided on yet another title for the band's American album. 'It will be called *Oompa-Loompa*.' (It won't.)

All three members of the band are looking forward to the challenge of getting the Busted name known out in the States, but right now they're not expecting any miracles when they jet over in the summer, and they know that nothing will come on a plate.

Having watched Busted's profile change in the UK over the last eighteen months, Charlie has another angle on his mind. 'For me, I don't want to have to fight the same old battles that we fought in the UK,' he says. 'I don't want the same old bullshit trying to convince people that we're not idiots. If people believe us from the word go, and if we don't have the same struggle that we've had here in the UK, we'll be fine. I think American audiences can be a lot more open to the idea of pop bands who play their instruments.' He sighs. 'We'll just have to wait and see.'

Nestling among the gifts in the dressing room at the Glasgow SECC is a presentation box containing something called a Universal Star Listing. Some fans have registered a star on Busted's behalf, and it has the co-ordinates Aquila 19h06m48s +6°36'59'. Nobody has much idea what this string of numbers and times might mean, but it's fair to say that the star, called Year 3000, is reasonably far away.

Inside the box is a note.

Hey, guys. Hope this gets to you in one piece, and I hope you like it. Congrats on your well-deserved Brits and your number ones and your several thousand awards. Matt, you are a brilliant bassist and my inspiration. I got a pic of mine – neat, huh? (A photograph is included, picturing a blue bass guitar surrounded by photos of Dougie from McFly.) Please say 'Hi' to Dougie, Tom, Danny and Harry. See you soon,
Lots of love,
Candice.

Someone raises the question of whether some fans have taken to using Busted to get at McFly. Since McFly first appeared on record – joining Busted on a 'Crashed The Wedding' B-side last year – some commentators have been quick to assume that they have been

cashing in on Busted's success. The phrase 'Busted Juniors' has been thrown around a lot.

As James is quick to explain, there's no clash.

'As similar as some people might think the two bands are, we're not that similar at all. McFly is completely inspired by 60s and sometimes 50s music. There are chords you'd use in a McFly song, which you'd never use in a Busted song. It's only because we introduced McFly that people think we're similar.'

To be fair, I point out, as well as sharing songwriters, you do also share a record label and a management team.

'Yes, but you can look at it two ways. I think McFly is a good thing for Busted. Forget my involvement with their songs – McFly are simply very good. And they keep the trend for credible pop bands going. Our fans are McFly fans, which means McFly fans are our fans. They're in touch. They fit in the same category as us.'

So really, if you also share the same fans and fit into the same category, you're *not* that different, after all? (James hates questions like this, but it's fun to watch him becoming increasingly frustrated.)

'It's hard to explain, but I really think both bands can exist in their own right.' He thinks for a while. 'Take the bands Charlie listens to – he likes a lot of nu-metal bands. But they're not all the same. They're in the same *category*, but they've got their own *style*. It's like Britney and Christina – they're not the same artists.'

Of course, James has answered these questions a hundred times already. But Charlie – the Busted member perhaps least likely to automatically put his seal of approval on any cynical 'Busted Juniors' idea – is also quick to defend McFly. 'They're really nice guys,' he says, 'and I like them both personally and as musicians. What they do is good. They're quite similar to Busted, yes, but only in the sense that one guitar band is like another guitar band.

'I did have an argument with James at one point. He said, "They're absolutely nothing like Busted," and I was like, "I know – but to outsiders they're going to look like a cash-in." But what are you going to do? Our management had such great talent in Tom, who was left over from Busted after I got the job, they were hardly going to let him go somewhere else. McFly are cool by me.'

March 17

Glas-gow

In catering Matt, James and Charlie are flicking through a copy of the industry magazine *Music Week*. Each week they reproduce the full album and single charts and this week, particularly in the album chart, there has been an invasion of artists like Jamie Cullum and Katie Melua, as well as various grandparents' favourites. It all seems very strange. Busted decide to discuss the very essence of pop music. What is pop?

Matt: Pop music is what is in the charts, with a sound that makes something appropriate for the commercial market.

James: But is that the only distinction? Is that all it is? Are Radiohead the same as Westlife?

Matt: No. And I think the problem is that there's not that much good pop music out there.

James: Katie Melua has had a Number One album now, so she's pop, even though she makes music which old people like. At the Royal Variety Performance I was standing next to her in the line when the Queen shook her hand, and the Queen actually made a point of saying to her, 'I really like your music.' It's the kind of music nans like.

Matt: The other day I sat down and looked at the charts and realised how much I didn't like. I like the Scissor Sisters now...What else do I like? Not much, really.

James: It's changing, though. Slowly. And the more good music that gets in the chart, the less room there is in the Top Forty for crap.

Charlie: Matt, I think you've become a lot more selective recently.

Matt: You're right, and it's your fault. I find myself being old and grumpy now and it's you, Charlie, who's made me such a grumpy-guts. I find your views spouting out of my mouth. Before Busted I'd be, like, 'I don't really like that song very much.' Nowadays I'm going, 'That is bloody shit! That is bollocks! That is the worst thing I've ever heard!' And that's all down to you.

Charlie: I do like pop music when it's good pop music, but all that *Pop Idol* stuff...

Author: Has *Pop Idol* changed what it means to have a Number One in the pop charts? How did you feel when 'You Said No' was your first, 'Crashed The Wedding' was your second, and 'Who's David' was your third?

Charlie: Number One is still a great thing, obviously. But it has been cheapened by *Pop Idol*. It's good when you fight for a Number One. You can't just have, 'Oh, Gareth will definitely be Number One because he's been on TV for the last three months.' That's bollocks. It's so much better when there's a battle and you're really fighting the promotion.

Author: So do you think it's the marketing and the promotion that makes a Number One, then? Rather than the song?

Charlie: I think it's the whole package. The whole thing of going 3-2-1 on the charts with our first three singles was perfect. We've had a great label and a great fan base all the way through.

We're on the tour bus on our way back to the hotel when James flicks through his diary and seems concerned about one particular date: Monday, March 28, the day after the final night of the tour. On this day there are two, clashing appointments.

'One is a driving test,' he admits. 'The other is some studio time I've booked, because I'm itching to get some music down after a month on the road. I'd rather have free time to make music than to spend afternoons practising reversing around corners, you know what I mean?'

Are you ever going to take your test?

'Yes. I promised myself I'd pass my test by the time I was twenty-one, and, when I promise myself something, it happens.'

Man-chester

'There are Doritos here, but where is my Boursin cheese?'

Manchester's shows will be important for two reasons. Firstly, they're the biggest dates of the tour – there will be 14,000 fans here each night, in this massive place with an extra tier right round the top made of seats that seem to rise almost vertically from the lower balcony. There's also the small matter of Busted's big November releases – a live album and DVD, both of which will be recorded during the second Manchester show, tomorrow night. There can be no stage invaders, or misintroduced songs, or fluffed lines, or malfunctioning guitars, or injured knees.

'Don't you think,' Matt announces, 'that dressing rooms are the most depressing places ever?' The Manchester MEN Arena dressing room is on a similar scale to the arena itself – massive – but it's pretty lifeless. The walls are made of concrete blocks painted turquoise, the carpet is a brown-specked affair, the adjoining bathroom brings back unpleasant memories of school PE lessons, and the beige patterned throws concealing mundane sofas are, frankly, fooling nobody.

James's mop-haired friend Kyle is over from Wisconsin ('It's cold here,' he ponders, though to be fair he is wearing shorts) and his brother Nick is still on the tour. Right now Nick is on one of the sofas playing 'Sleeping With The Light On' on an acoustic guitar. Matt is trying his best to throw a diva strop, but with limited success.

'Look!' he shouts, waving his arms around at the rider and being ignored by everyone. 'There are Doritos here, but where is my Boursin cheese?' He begins muttering about how rubbish their rider has been, immediately conceding that it's entirely his own fault for not making any special requests. 'On our next tour,' Matt announces, 'we're going the whole hog. I'm having a KFC Bargain Bucket, with gravy.' A thought occurs to him. 'No! I want no "bargain" involved in my food! Get me a KFC Expensive Bucket! And I want my fries from somewhere else! Like...McDonalds!' And that, readers, is as demanding as Busted are ever likely to get.

Tonight's show is an opportunity for the band to acquaint themselves with the Manchester stage before the show is filmed tomorrow night and, back at the hotel bar, the lads seem happy with how the show went. Tonight the band really will have an early night – or relatively early, at any rate – in an attempt to save their voices for tomorrow night's cameras.

March 20

Man-chester

On DVD Day, Manchester is windy. So windy that, outside the arena, some fans are blown clean off their feet by an unexpected gust. In the dressing room, Matt is wearing the grey 'Punk Fakes' T-shirt – last seen when Busted were on the cover of the *Observer Music Monthly* magazine in a piece attempting to claim that, along with artists like the Sugababes, Busted were at the forefront of a new Britpop revolution. 'You won't be at all surprised to hear that my throat is buggered,' he moans. 'It was fine, and then it wasn't, and then it was fine again, and then...' He sprays something down his throat, and gags. 'That hasn't helped. I might as well have gone out and got really pissed last night for all the good a decent night's sleep has done.' He goes on to explain that the tour has already claimed another casualty: last night, in the hotel bar, Busted's press officer Heather had been attempting to recreate some boyband dance moves, managed to rupture a tendon in her leg and was last seen being stretchered out of the hotel and into the back of an ambulance.

It's time to shoot some backstage footage for the DVD, so everyone's ushered out of the dressing room for a short while. On the way out, Adam Lambert asks the cameraman whether he wants a guitar – which is on the coffee table along with a load of spent water bottles – in shot.

'Yeah,' says the cameraman. 'Let's have a bit of rock'n'roll.'

'Rock'n'roll.' Adam laughs. 'An acoustic guitar and some empty Evian bottles.'

McFly are just arriving, having only recently stepped off a plane from London, where they've been recording a performance for *CD:UK*. The wind, they say, was so bad that the turbulence was the worst any of them have ever experienced, and the pilot had to abandon one landing and try again. Two members of the band admit that they fully expected to die on the second attempt.

We walk out to inspect the arena and find a higher concentration of cameras than you'd get in your average *Big Brother* house – there are eleven attached to the front of the stage, all pointing at slightly different parts of the stage, and loads more have been positioned around the arena, which is freezing cold.

James, meanwhile, is telling Fletch and Richard about a guy he met in the hotel bar last night – an up-and-coming songwriter currently in a band called Dudefish. The name 'Dudefish' provokes some uncertain glances around the table. 'I think it's a cool name!' James protests. 'You're not going to forget it, are you. Ask me in two years the name of that guy's band, and I'll say, "The band's name was Dudefish."' James suggests that Fletch and Richard should meet the Dudefish dude, because his songs were really good.

'He likes the same bands as me, and he hates the same bands as me,' James continues. 'He played me some of his tracks – there was a great one called "I'm A Loser And A Clown".' I ask whether James sees a future for himself in artist management. He nods. 'Maybe. But there's a lot of other stuff I want to do first.'

Backstage before the gig, the dressing room is in pandemonium: assorted people from the band's label have dropped in with their kids to say hello, and Matt, Charlie and Fletch are having a meeting in the toilet. On emerging from his meeting Matt discovers that yesterday's Boursin has finally arrived, and begins to eat it out of the wrapper.

Showtime comes around quickly. Because it's being recorded, the lads' between-song banter is tempered slightly, and there's an awkward moment during Charlie's solo song 'Why' when his guitar fails. After the band have performed 'Fake', someone scuttles on stage from the wings and whispers something in James's ear. 'Now

'This is going to look a bit stupid,' he warns, 'but pretend to go mental anyway. Again.'

there's something you don't see every day,' Matt comments. 'That was our manager, Fletch.' It turns out that Charlie will be redoing 'Why' for the benefit of the DVD, so when James and Matt leave the stage he's charged with the slightly embarrassing duty of telling the audience. 'This is going to look a bit stupid,' he warns, 'but pretend to go mental anyway. Again.'

Afterwards, Matt appears with a camcorder – for the DVD – and lightens the mood a little by indulging in 'something which I know is really really cheesy' (but looks really really cool) when he brings the lights down and counts down for every audience member with a camera to let the flash off at once. It's the cheapskate's approach to pyrotechnics, but it looks amazing. Matt seems chuffed, thanks the audience, tosses the camera off stage to a waiting pair of hands and resumes the show.

Because the boys are running – sprinting straight from the stage and into a waiting tourbus – after tonight's show, we're already on the tour bus by the time they hop aboard, and the journey back to the Lowry only takes about five minutes. Freshening up in his room, Charlie recalls that, when Busted stayed here during last year's theatre tour, they were shocked to discover that a Bar Mitzvah party had also been booked at the hotel. This meant that plenty of teenagers were staying in the hotel, and the band's after-show drinks were punctuated every couple of minutes by autograph-signing sessions. Charlie seems relieved that this time round the band are guaranteed a bit of a chance to unwind. We get in the lift and descend to the bar on the ground floor. The doors ping open and dozens of pairs of teenage eyes turn to Charlie. This time there is not one Bar Mitzvah taking place at the Lowry, but two.

We find a quiet corner and are joined by the footballer Wayne Rooney, who has a good chat with Matt before we bid farewell and decamp to a bar called Tiger Tiger, which is just around the corner. On the way, Matt mentions that Wayne was in the audience tonight and says that the reports are good: Wayne enjoyed the show. 'To be honest, the first time I met him I really wanted to be his mate.' Matt laughs. 'I was like, "It's bloody Wayne Rooney!" But I got really shy. I met him after an England–Slovakia match once. He took his England shirt off his back, and signed it "To Matt, Best Wishes, Wayne Rooney".' Matt laughs again – at one of the Wembley shows, England rugby captain Laurence Dallaglio had been in Woody's Bar for the after-show and presented Matt with a signed England rugby shirt. Matt pulls at his black Fred Perry top. 'I don't think taking this off, signing it and handing it over to an international sportsman would really have the same effect, would it. Plus, nobody would want this after I've come off stage. I'm rubbish at being star struck.'

Does the feeling of being star struck mean that you have more of a perspective of what it's like for a Busted fan when you sign an autograph?

'Yes.' He thinks for a while. 'Yes, sometimes I suppose that is true.'

What with it being a Saturday night in Manchester, Tiger Tiger is rammed, but the management have roped off an area for the Busted tour party in one corner of the very top floor. There are so many of us here that our area ends up being more squashed than anywhere else in the club, but all that is forgotten when the booze arrives. And continues to arrive. And keeps on coming. Only when the bar closes are there less drinks on the table than there are members of the party and, as the Tiger Tiger staff begin wiping down the bar, Matt decides that it is time to showcase his skills as a barman. His novel approach to the art of cocktail making – take whatever spirits are to hand and chuck them in a glass with no mixer – leaves everyone reeling, and it's time for bed.

March 26

London: Part Two

We're back at Wembley for the second series of London dates, and the final shows of the tour. Since we last saw the band they've played another Sheffield date and two in Birmingham, but there are three gigs to go this weekend – one tonight, one tomorrow and one on Sunday. The DVD and album have been recorded; anyone who's going to review the show has already been, and already it's feeling as if the tour is winding down, so the boys are more keen than ever not to let complacency set in. Not that they have much chance to rest on their laurels today – they'll be busy with another set of interviews, and at 5.30 p.m. there will be a private screening, in the boys' dressing room, of the *Thunderbirds* movie.

Charlie already has other things on his mind. Yesterday he picked up his new car, a vehicle so crammed with state-of-the-art gadgetry and gizmos that someone from the showroom spent yesterday morning showing Charlie how to work it. 'It's got all the Bluetooth stuff for my phone, and a TV, and lots of different electrical buttons,' Charlie enthuses, beaming. 'And it's got satellite navigation, which is amazing. Say I'm going to the Barfly in Glasgow. You type in "Barfly, Glasgow", and it takes you there. Which is good because I'm so shit at map reading. The tyres are amazing. It's like driving a spaceship.'

What's it like driving a spaceship? 'Bloody cool.'

First up today is the soundcheck. Watching from the empty auditorium, a passing roadie notes with some amusement that, after a few weeks of dragging their heels during these afternoon run-throughs, Matt, James and Charlie seem genuinely to be enjoying their time on stage this afternoon.

In the dressing room it is mentioned that, this morning, tickets went on sale for the London dates of Madonna's 2004 tour. Concert ticket prices are all pretty steep these days, but Madonna's are unusually pricey, ranging from £50 to £160.

Charlie pokes his head around the bathroom door, toothbrush sticking out of his mouth, looking utterly appalled. 'Each?'

Yes.

'That's an absolute joke. I thought the same thing when the Rolling Stones played and their tickets were £150. Actually mine weren't because I got them cheaper. But that's not the point. You've got to see the full picture – perhaps they're doing it for tax reasons or something – but, if they're doing it just because they can, that's messed up. She's already got loads of money.'

How much would you pay to see Madonna?

'Three pounds. And that would have to include the booking fee. Fair dos to her and she's obviously good at what she does, but I really have no interest in anything she does.'

Also this week, James's brother Nick has been 'papped' for the first time, appearing in one of the tabloid papers with James in a record shop. Now, it's fair to say that Nick – who's appeared in the 'You Said No', 'Who's David' and 'Air Hostess' videos – doesn't mind having his face on camera, but he did find the experience a bit weird, especially since he says today that the first he knew of the picture being taken was when it actually turned up in the paper.

Matt has also been photographed recently – wandering down the street with a Sid Vicious poster – and has his own plans. 'I'm going to start a side project with a mate,' he confides as he munches on yet another packet of Boursin cheese. 'He's skint, so what we're going to do is set up some paparazzi shots of me doing things like falling over, buying some chips, breathing or whatever, and then he can flog them to magazines. He'll be minted!'

We mention the bar of eBay soap from earlier in the tour. By this point the auction has been mysteriously

withdrawn, meaning that the winning bidders never received their Busted pube-and-soap parcel. But Matt has ideas for this, too. 'The plan is that I'm going to get all these little things signed by the band, and then the same mate can go off and sell them. It might as well be one of my friends who profits from it.'

At 7 p.m., Busted emerge from their *Thunderbirds* screening. The boys had seen some rough cuts of the film last winter when they'd initially been approached to write the song, but this is the first time any of them had seen the whole thing, and it was an opportunity to see whether the film was any good. James seems happy.

'As soon as I heard we were doing the song I went out and bought all the old videos, and having watched those what's good about this film is how true they've stayed to the characters. It's not a teen movie, it's not a "fifteen", it's a family movie. But you can count any number of family movies which are brilliant films.'

He counts about twelve and then gives up.

Tonight's show passes almost without incident. At one point, before 'She Wants To Be Me', Matt checks the set list and then pauses. 'I can't believe it's the third-to-last night of the tour,' he says, lauging, 'and I'm still checking the set list.' Before 'Britney', James follows his usual 'She's got diamonds on her titties' comment with '...in her new video', as if there is likely to be any suspicion in the audience's mind that Britney Spears wears a diamond breast adornment when she's putting the bins out. Towards the end of the song Matt and James miss their cues, sending Matt into fits of hysterics.

In tonight's jumping-through-a-hole-in-the-floor finale, Charlie manages to hit his head on the side of the stage. He is fine, but sees fit to turn the whole thing into a drama and insists on sympathy from everyone in the dressing room. 'You know,' Matt says afterwards, 'it's going to be weird playing small venues again.'

March 27

London: Part Two

'Paul Weller,' James notes, 'is not just a star. He's a megastar.'

Last night, Matt spent an evening in the company of Lee Ryan from Blue, and when he crawls into Wembley Arena at 3 p.m. is feeling understandably the worse for wear. During the soundcheck James's voice is also suffering but watching from one side is Charlie's 24-year-old brother, Will. Will is the Simpson brother who doesn't look like the other two, and he co-wrote the *A Present For Everyone* song 'Why'. 'It was a song I wrote when I was seventeen,' Will explains. 'Last year Charlie asked if he could have a play around with it. He rocked it up a bit and when he'd finished he asked if I minded the song going on the second Busted album. I was like, "Of course you can."'

Will didn't realise that agreeing to this meant that, when it came to the arena tour, he'd be invited up on stage at Wembley to perform the song. 'I could hardly refuse,' he says, laughing, 'but right now, on a scale of one to ten, I'm eight-out-of-ten nervous. This soundcheck will be the first time I've actually played the song properly with Charlie, but I'm really looking forward to it.'

Will was also at the first Wembley date the other week, and remembers how impressed he was to see his little brother shoot up from below the stage for the first song. 'I can't believe that for my eighteen-year-old brother this is just another day at Wembley.' He smiles. 'It's crazy to think that he's a pro at this now. He'd only been to one band audition before Busted. He got down to the final eight and didn't get in, so when the Busted audition came up he said, "This is the last audition I'm doing," which is so typical of Charlie's lack of patience. He got down to the final twenty and then when he got to the final five we all started to think, Oh my word.'

Has he changed much in the last two years?

'As a person, no. He's still got the same humour and he's the same guy. I wouldn't say he was shy before, he's a lot more confident now. He believes in himself now.' He laughs. 'He's also become a little more lazy.'

In the dressing room, Matt decides to impress us with a card trick. 'Right,' he begins, shuffling the pack. 'Pick any card from the pack. Take a look at it but don't let me see.' He shuffles the pack again, and splits it in four, arranging each at right angles. 'Now pick one of these four quarters.' We go for the second one down. 'Put your card into that pack. Now put those cards between one of the three other quarters I have in my hand.' He shuffles the pack for a minute and then, with a flourish, picks one from the pack. It's the eight of hearts. 'Was this your card?'

No.

'I didn't think it would be. I can't do any card tricks.'

Tonight's meet-and-greet – the penultimate one of the tour – is the most chaotic so far. As soon as Matt, James and Charlie walk into Woody's Bar there's a scream, and for the next twenty minutes they are pulled and pushed from fan to fan, grabbed by parents and herded around like cattle. Afterwards, Charlie is slightly dazed. 'Meeting fans is brilliant,' he begins, 'but some of those kids weren't even fans. One of them came up to me and went, "Which one are you? Are you James?"'

To illustrate his rage, Charlie picks a banana from the fruit bowl and breaks it in half while making a reasonably manly noise.

'Ooh.' Matt laughs. '*That* was scary.'

Matt goes for a half-hour nap on the bus and, when he returns, is informed that legendary rocker Paul Weller will be in tonight's audience, having brought his kids along to see the band. 'Paul Weller,' James notes, 'is not just a star. He's a megastar.' In spite of Weller's slump into dadrock territory over the last few years, he remains one of Matt's idols and he scours the venue trying to find Weller. He doesn't have to look far – he's in Woody's Bar. Matt runs back. 'Come on, guys – let's go and look at Paul Weller!'

After the show, Charlie announces for the first time in three weeks that he is hungry. There are startled expressions. 'Do you know what?' Charlie asks to anyone who'll listen. 'I haven't been eating on this tour. Halfway through the tour I realised I was too tired to eat. I got on the scales this morning and I've lost over a stone in the space of a month. I've been living on crisps and Haribo.'

March 28

London: Part Two

'It doesn't come much more rock'n'roll than that,' comments the soundman.

Richard Rashman appears to be asleep in the dressing room, though he will later insist that he was merely resting his eyes. You couldn't blame him for grabbing forty winks, though – it has been a long tour and today we will all lose count of how many times the phrase 'last day of school' is used.

'I feel like the most unhealthy person in the world,' Matt moans as he flings himself onto a dressing-room sofa. 'Every single part of my body feels like shit.' He looks in the mirror. 'OH MY GOD. I've been hanging around James so long that I'm beginning to take on his facial expressions.'

For Matt, it seems the end of the tour has not come a moment too soon. 'I really am shattered,' he continues. 'I've had so much fun over the last month that I really need it to finish. I probably haven't had more late nights this time round than I did on the last tour – it's just that this time round I've left the hotel bar and seen the bars of local areas. It's been more of a *cultural* tour.'

James arrives looking sheepish. Last night he had arrived home, walked to his front door and realised that his keys were still in the dressing room; he had to come all the way back and ask to be allowed back in so that he could find them. Matt's still buzzing from Paul Weller being in last night's audience. 'Often when I meet people I want to impress, I am a twat.' He grins. 'Last night I was that twat. It was like Wayne Rooney all over again. Paul Weller was there, man. He looked like the coolest dude in the world. Charlie actually asked him what he thought of the show. And he replied, "It was all right. You do what you do." Which was neither here nor there. It was polite. I think he just thought, Look, don't think I'm here to see you – I'm here because my daughter wants to see you. Which is cool, because he's Paul Weller and he can do what he wants.'

During the soundcheck, Charlie nips off stage and sits in the front row. 'So this is what it feels like to watch Busted on stage,' he says with a smile. Imagine Busted are on stage right now, I suggest. 'OK,' he agrees. After a while, he decides: 'That was very cool.' He gets up and jumps back on stage to continue the soundcheck.

On each soundcheck of the tour, during downtime, the band have treated the guys on the sound deck to an impromptu cover version. Since it's the last day of the tour, they're taking requests.

'What do you want to hear today?' asks Chris Banks.

A voice booms back from the sound desk: 'I'll leave that up to you. It's the last day of school.'

The band strike up a rendition of Guns N' Roses' 'Sweet Child O' Mine'. The sound-desk voice booms back once more: 'Just don't do any Guns N' Roses songs.' Now the band launch into a bit of 'You Said No'. 'It doesn't come much more rock'n'roll than that,' comments the soundman.

'Yes it does,' mutters Damon, and as if to disprove his theory the band begin to rattle through 'Money For Nothing' by 80s rockers Dire Straits.

After the soundcheck, Charlie relaxes in his seat. Tomorrow Charlie will be moving house; his current home is full of boxes and, more pressingly, a number of items not yet in boxes will somehow need to be packed by the time a man arrives with a van tomorrow morning.

'I think tonight is a good night to end the tour,' he announces.

Well, it is the final date, so it couldn't really be more ideal.

'Yes,' he agrees. 'Exactly.'

What with it being the last day of school, there are various plans afoot for comedy pranks to be played on stage tonight. James, professional as ever, is not so sure this a good idea. 'The last show has to be the best show,' he announces.

'We're not doing a pantomime. It's really important to try and make each show brilliant.' He remembers one night of the tour, early on when his voice had gone, when he was so frustrated that he actually sat down on stage during 'She Wants To Be Me'. 'I was so pissed off,' he remembers. 'I hated every minute of it. I feel like I've spent the rest of the tour making up for that.'

James's suggested ban on high jinks hasn't totally dampened the spirits. Guitarist Chris has hatched a plan to scrawl expletives on every single piece of Damon's drum kit. It will, we are assured, be hilarious.

In the dressing room, wrappers and cans and bags and rubbish are strewn everywhere; banana skins overflow from polystyrene cups and Haribo line the floor. We discuss the news that Flawless, one member of the six-strong UK urban pop act Big Brovaz, has been thrown out of the band. On a promotional trip to the States, Flawless had been stopped at customs and found with a small amount of cannabis in his bag. 'Well, there *were* six of them,' Charlie reasons, with typical Simpson logic. 'They probably won't miss him.'

An hour before Busted are due on stage to perform their final show, concert promoter Simon Moran appears at the dressing-room door with gifts from his company – one-of-a-kind (or at least three-of-a-kind) Busted flight cases full of goodies, framed tour posters (with 'SOLD OUT' stamped in huge letters across every single date), and bottles of champagne. The framed posters come as a relief to Charlie, since a similar poster presented at the end of the last tour has been accidentally smashed. 'You don't need the old one anyway,' James sniffs. 'This one's bigger and better.'

Damon appears. 'Someone has written rude words all over every single one of my skins.' He hasn't noticed that someone has also written 'Argos' very neatly on the front of his very expensive, definitely-not-from-Argos drum kit.

James and Matt are discussing a new Busted song they've written. The problem, Matt says, is that it doesn't sound very Busted-ish. James decides that the song needs a rap, and performs it in full on his acoustic guitar, singing the rap from Coolio's 'Gangsta's Paradise' over the top. Seemingly unimpressed, Matt floats the idea of taking it round to Lee Ryan's house for some extra work – when he was round there the other night, Matt had been surprised by the number of good tracks Lee had written. There was one slightly awkward moment, however. 'Lee played me this one song which was just amazing,' Matt explains. 'A really massive ballad with strong, really emotive vocals. I was like, "This is brilliant – it should be a single." He looked a bit confused and went, "Er, it *is* a single. It's 'Breathe Easy'. It was out last week."'

For the last time until this summer's outdoor shows, the boys strap on those damned head mics and get ready to go on stage. 'Let's walk out together properly tonight,' Matt says. 'Let's get it right.'

'I want to have a group prayer!' James guffaws. 'We haven't done a group prayer all tour!'

They don't have one tonight, either.

True to James's demands, tonight's really is one of the best shows of the entire tour, with storming, top-form performances from every single musician on stage, and a suitably appreciative response from an audience who clearly sense the significance and, at times, emotion of the show. Matt's mates – still shouting 'RUDE BOY!' above the noise of the rest of their block – are back in the audience.

In Woody's after the show, the atmosphere is unbelievable. No tears for the end of the tour, just a huge feeling of pride and accomplishment on a job well done.

'Well,' says James, beer in hand, 'that's the arena tour done. It's quite cool to be able to say that. Let's go and get pissed.'

March 28

After 24 dates, 10 cities, a quarter of a million tickets sold, 7 kilograms of Haribo, one broken television and countless minor injuries, the tour is finally over.

We jump in the Busted tour bus for one last time. It hasn't played host to this many people all tour – downstairs passengers spill from the seats, cram into the stairwell and even shut themselves in the toilet in an attempt to squeeze in; upstairs every bunk is full and the corridor is packed with people. As we sway our way through north London to the final after-show party, James reflects on the gig. 'I'm not really an "emotional last night" type of person,' he admits, 'but I enjoyed soaking up that feeling for one last time. As soon as I get out of bed tomorrow there will still be a million other things going on, and there'll be a million other things the day after that. But I'm never going to forget this tour.'

The bus grinds to a halt. We've arrived at our destination – the Eve club, on Regent Street in the heart of London. Eve is great for two reasons. Firstly because, in the 1960s, it was central to a massive Government sex scandal; secondly, and more importantly, because it has an illuminated dance floor.

Drink is free and the tunes are cheesy. 'Year 3000' packs the floor. Everyone dances. Some people fall over. One person bursts into tears. After 24 dates, 10 cities, a quarter of a million tickets sold, 7 kilograms of Haribo, one broken television and countless minor injuries, the tour is finally over.

At the end of the year, the band will do it all over again. Dates are already selling out for the band's 'A Ticket For Everyone Else' tour. In the corner of the dance floor, James mentions rumours he's heard that this tour will be the band's last. He laughs. 'The funny thing,' he shouts above the roar of OutKast's 'Hey Ya!', 'and the thing that some people don't realise, is that when we're on stage we have as good a time, if not a better time, than the fans do. That's just the way it is. If they want us here, we'll be here. We're not ready for a farewell tour. We haven't even really begun yet.'

As he staggers to his taxi, Matt has the very final word. 'This is what it's all been about,' he shouts. 'This is what being in Busted is ALL about. Playing live is everything.'

He falls into the cab.

FLANNELS

Discography

WHAT I GO TO SCHOOL FOR
SINGLE PROMO

WHAT I GO TO SCHOOL FOR
SINGLE CD1

16TH SEPTEMBER 2002
03

WHAT I GO TO SCHOOL FOR
SINGLE CD2

16TH SEPTEMBER 2002
03

BUSTED ALBUM
ALBUM

30TH SEPTEMBER 2002
01

YEAR 3000
SINGLE PROMO

YEAR 3000
SINGLE CD1

13TH JANUARY 2003
02

YEAR 3000
SINGLE CD2

13TH JANUARY 2003
02

YOU SAID NO
SINGLE PROMO

YOU SAID NO
SINGLE CD1

21ST APRIL 2003
01

YOU SAID NO
SINGLE CD2

21ST APRIL 2003
01

SLEEPING WITH THE LIGHT ON
SINGLE PROMO

SLEEPING WITH THE LIGHT ON
SINGLE CD1

11TH AUGUST 2003
04

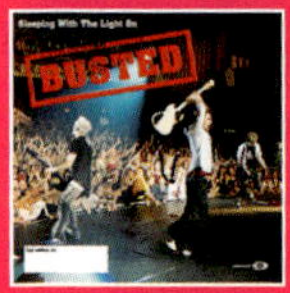

SLEEPING WITH THE LIGHT ON
SINGLE CD2

11TH AUGUST 2003
04

CRASHED THE WEDDING
SINGLE PROMO

CRASHED THE WEDDING
SINGLE CD1

10TH NOVEMBER 2003
01

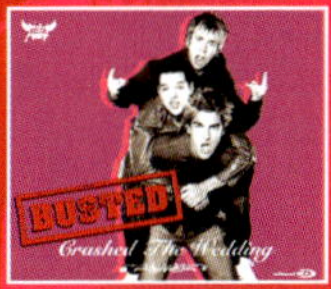

CRASHED THE WEDDING
SINGLE CD2

10TH NOVEMBER 2003
01

A PRESENT FOR EVERYONE
ALBUM

17TH NOVEMBER 2003
02

WHO'S DAVID
SINGLE PROMO

WHO'S DAVID
SINGLE CD1

16TH FEBRUARY 2004
01

WHO'S DAVID
SINGLE CD2

16TH FEBRUARY 2004
01

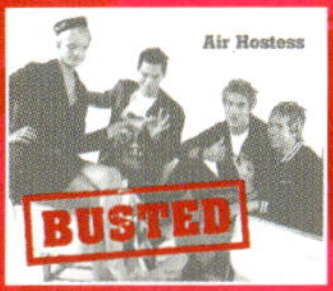

AIR HOSTESS
PROMO

AIR HOSTESS
SINGLE CD1

26TH APRIL 2004
02

AIR HOSTESS
SINGLE CD2

26TH APRIL 2004
02

AIR HOSTESS
SINGLE 7"

26TH APRIL 2004
02

THUNDERBIRDS/3am
SINGLE CD1

26TH JULY 2004

3am/THUNDERBIRDS
SINGLE CD2

26TH JULY 2004

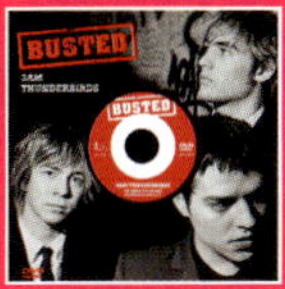

3am/THUNDERBIRDS
SINGLE DVD

26TH JULY 2004

BUSTED